TERRORISM: WTF?
WEAPONS, TACTICS & THE FUTURE

AN IN-DEPTH LOOK AT THE PEOPLE,
MOTIVATIONS, TACTICS, AND FUTURE
OF TERRORISM

AUDREY   DAVID
CASSERLEIGH & MERRICK
FLORIDA STATE UNIVERSITY

Kendall Hunt
publishing company

Cover design by Jarrett Broder

Kendall Hunt
publishing company

www.kendallhunt.com
Send all inquiries to:
4050 Westmark Drive
Dubuque, IA 52004-1840

Copyright © 2013 by Kendall Hunt Publishing Company

ISBN 978-1-4652-3490-2

Printed in the United States of America
10 9 8 7 6 5 4 3 2 1

Contents

Foreword

Seriously, WTF is terrorism? The term is used so often everyone seems to be a terrorist, fighting terrorism, harboring terrorists, or terrorizing someone. And since time never stops, we are further away from landmark terror events every day, which can dim recollection and muddle understanding. Not a day goes by where we don't stare at the TV or a website and mutter, "you got it wrong . . . again." Despite the fact that we have lived with the "War on Terror" for the past twelve years, many of us still don't understand what is happening. Our courses (and this text) aim to change that.

There's a saying in academics that students get younger every year, which is just jab at aging professors. Our students are still in their dawn of adulthood, but our age gaps are now measured in decades and cultural centuries. Many of the readers of this text will have been young children during 9/11—the shocking domestic event that is still perpetrating changes to the American way of life. For younger students of this text there is no "before 9/11," only the world now, so WTF is terrorism, and why is it relevant? (We might answer that question, but more importantly terrorism is just really interesting, so read the rest of the book.)

This text was written for our students and is a gift they never wanted, but needed. Because we know and love our students we may occasionally swerve onto the soapbox and start lecturing in a completely biased and un-neutral way. We will do our best to let you know when this happens, setting our spurious opinions away from the actual text.

If we haven't lost you yet with our ramblings, indulge us for another minute with dedications:

From Audrey:

To my family who know me, and despite that, continue to love me. Without you my ego would not fit through doorways, and my heart would be empty.

To Dean Rasmussen, the best type of boss; he gives us just enough rope to hang ourselves, gracefully insulates us from drama, and laughs in all the right places.

And, to our staff, the bravest band of genius goofballs ever to build a jello-like dynasty. You make work a joy, Fridays a blessing, and infections rampant.

From David:

This book is dedicated to Holly, David and Chase, who have given up weekends, evenings and family dinners so I could lock myself in my office to work. Thank you, and know that I love you even when sleep deprived and cranky!

To my coworkers, thank you for all your hard work day in and day out. Nothing would be working without all your efforts.

One last note: Like coroners at a convention our humor is morbid, dark, and dry. We take our research and this topic very seriously (mostly) but believe that levity and laughter facilitate better learning. We hope humor will provide an alternative emotion to the overwhelming grimness that accompanies terrorism and acts of extraordinary violence. It may be that our purpose in life is to serve as a warning to others, so judge the authors at will, disagree and grimace, just promise you will think, question, ponder, evaluate, learn . . . and maybe laugh.

Audrey and David
May 2013

Chapter 1

Defining Terrorism

The core of the issue of defining terrorism is the freedom fighter vs. terrorism issue stated in the common phrase, "One man's terrorist is another man's freedom fighter." Stated more obviously—if you believe in what they're blowing up/destroying/attacking, you don't think they're terrorists. This question of perspective, and who is the enemy, is as old as conflict itself. No one joins a cause and thinks, "I am the enemy, and I'm looking forward to fighting the hero!"

One of the grandfathers of terrorism research, Walter Laqueur, asks if in certain circumstances terrorism might be a legitimate form of resistance against tyranny. This question has particular relevance as we explore the changing boundaries of what is defined as terrorism.

The contemporary problem with defining terrorism is the overuse of the word. When we throw around the terms *terrorism*, *terrorists*, *terrorizing*, we make it difficult to understand the specific character of what terrorism really is. Overuse, or inappropriate use, of the term inflates statistics, makes us immune to the term, and confuses the world to the issues at hand. Our tolerance toward terrorism changes as we become desensitized to the word.

Gus Martin's work in observing and defining terrorism in the modern contexts notes that terrorism today is understood to involve loose, cell-based networks that wage politically motivated, asymmetrical violence against non-military targets. Martin's work turns the focus on the structure and the target of the organization rather than the purpose of the action.

When was the Term Terrorism First Used?

The term *terrorism* was originally coined by Maximillian Robespierre during the Reign of Terror, a period associated with the French Revolution. Robespierre was

What is the inherent problem with Lacquer's question regarding legitimate terrorism?

In theory, if there is real tyranny occurring, a small terror group should not be the only ones recognizing or acting against it. In the cases of real tyranny, like you might find under a dictator, shouldn't the world audience recognize it as such and come to the aid of those being tyrannized?

What is the inherent problem with Martin's definition regarding terrorism?

The structure of an organization should not be a determining factor in defining terrorism, Martin's reference to cell-based structures would preclude the single actors or "lone wolf" phenomena. If terrorists have to be part of a cell-based structure then neither Richard Reid the shoe bomber, nor Major Hasan the Fort Hood shooter, could be called terrorists.

careful to emphasize that terrorism was the combination of violence with purpose, and famously said in 1793,

> *If the spring of popular government in time of peace is virtue, the springs of popular government in revolution are at once virtue and terror:* **virtue***, without which terror is fatal; terror, without which virtue is powerless. Terror is nothing other than justice, prompt, severe, inflexible.*

The use of the term *terrorism* during this period had a positive connotation and was embraced to describe revolutionary actions. Robespierre even went so far as to recommend terrorism as a systematic tool in reaching the goals of the state.

What is interesting about the birth of this word is the combination of *virtue* and *terror*. Without question, terror just for the sake of fear, without purpose and just to kill, is not terrorism. Recent violent acts, like the 2012 Aurora movie theatre shooting where a single gunman killed 12 people, or the 2012 Sandy Hook school shooting, which killed 28 people, 20 of which were children, were *random acts of extraordinary violence*. They were perpetrated by lone gunmen, who were mentally unhealthy, with no purpose or political motivation. These random acts of extraordinary violence had no virtue; they were not intended to serve as a tool for change, the targets were not symbolic of a regime or government or political body. These acts did not draw attention to a plight or injustice and were terrifying and criminal and horrific, but not terrorism.

Please do not mistake our passion for defining terrorism as advocacy for violence. We will talk in later chapters about mitigating, preventing, and stopping terrorism. We only ask that as you evaluate what is terrorism, you consider and evaluate the whole, which is greater than the sum of its parts.

Defining Terrorists by Attitude

Defining terrorism is a challenge globally, not just in this text. The **United Nations** has been convening world leaders for decades to try and solve this riddle of perspective vs. actions. Former Secretary General of the United Nations, Kofi Annan, made defining what constitutes terrorism one of the priorities of his tenure. Specifically, in the post 9/11 era, the UN wanted to bridge the gap between acts of extraordinary violence and the concern raised by the Islamic Organization Countries that, a single definition might blur the difference between terrorism and the legitimate struggle against foreign occupation. The result of the UN's efforts, the 2006 report Uniting Against Terrorism-Recommendations for a Global Counter-Terrorism Strategy focused on the **moral aspects of terrorism** that focus on hyper nationalistic and xenophobic messages that glorify mass murder and martyrdom.

This is a stunning perspective because instead of focusing on politics like Laqueur, or organization like Martin, the UN council emphasized attitude and beliefs. The *hyper nationalistic* (a fervent love of your own nation) and *xenophobic* (hatred of others who are different from you) emphasis on psychological or personality traits is a very interesting focus for a terrorism definition! If you look at just those traits, you find people of every culture who are hyper nationalistic (In the United States imagine people who dress up as Uncle Sam on 4ᵗʰ of July) and are xenophobic (in the United States think the KKK). It is only when you combine these **psychological traits** with acts of **extraordinary violence**, you do get a unique and interesting attempt at defining terrorists.

The UN and its member states still have no agreed-upon definition, and this continues to be a problem when discussing international counterterrorism agendas and programs. Without a definition, world leaders (and terrorists) agree upon it is difficult to pursue anti-terror partnerships. An example of the power of a UN definition can be found in the Geneva Convention's 1949 "Protection of Civilian Persons in a Time of War," which prevents the "mutilation, cruel treatment, and torture" of prisoners and noncombatants. The Geneva Convention has been used as a foundation for persecuting war criminals in the Hague International Criminal Courts, and if an agreed upon definition of terrorism were made a similar process could exist.

Ok, But What if they're Crazy?

Another prominent issue is the differentiation of terrorism from by those who have little mental stability or who may just be criminals. In some circles researchers even argue that crimes do terrorize, so wouldn't criminals be terrorists. . . .?

The distinction between a criminal act and a terrorist act can often be found in the result of the actions. A criminal act is done for profit, with the perpetrator seeking some sort of personal goal, while a terrorist act has the goal of change through fear or intimidation. In general most definitions shun the idea of terrorism as simply a criminal act and focuses on terrorism as a tool for political change. It is sometimes noted that the presence of terrorism in a society can be an indicator that society is too rigid and locked down to be modified with normal political instruments. The presence of terrorism as a political tool may also mean there are problems inherent to that society the public may not have been aware of.

If change is the goal of violent action in terrorism the violent action alone is not terrorism

Change movement + violence = terrorism
Personal profit + violence = criminal
Violence ≠ terrorism
Change movement ≠ terrorism
Personal profit ≠ terrorism

When violence is conducted intentionally the mental status of the perpetrator is evaluated. Mental status directly affects understanding and motivation, and vice versa. If a violent perpetrator is considered mentally unstable, we perceive and evaluate the violence within a different rubric. Very rarely have acts of terrorism been undertaken by a mentally unstable individuals.

Theodore Kaczynski had difficulty integrating into society as an adult, but was by all accounts a brilliant mathematician. Working as a math professor in his early 20s Kaczynski seemed to suffer a severe mental break, resulting in a decision to remove himself from society entirely. He self-isolated himself off the grid in Montana and began an anonymous letter-writing campaign to several perceived enemies, including the U.S. government, the entertainment industry, and corporate technology.

At some point in his late 20s Kaczynski began anonymously sending bombs in the mail to several universities and airline companies, earning the FBI file name UNiversity and Airline Bomber or UNABOMBER. For the next 15 years Kaczynski continued to send anonymous bombs to a random assortment of perceived enemies. He embraced his own nickname and would occasionally include messages in his devices signed from the UNABOMBER. The bombs increased in lethality over time, ultimately resulting in 23 injuries and three deaths, before Kaczynski was caught. It was not until the UNABOMBER demanded that one of his manifestos be published by the media that Kaczynski's brother recognized the writing, ultimately leading the FBI to the Montana hermit.

Despite being labeled criminally insane, Kaczynski refused to acknowledge any of his mental health deficits and eventually entered a plea deal as a domestic terrorist. Currently in prison Kaczynski has undergone extensive psychological assessments and has been diagnosed as a paranoid schizophrenic. This disorder often manifests itself during early adulthood and could help to explain Kaczynski's highly unusual and violent behavior.

We Overuse the Term . . . Because We Don't Know What it Means

The attempt to understand the universality of terrorism transcends the theoretical boundaries of discussions and is more than an exercise in conceptualization. The lack of a consistent definition creates an environment where it is impossible to formulate or enforce agreements against terrorism or understand the use of extraordinary violence that is the hallmark of terrorism. Without a real, usable, and agreed-upon definition we have begun overutilizing the word *terrorism* to the point of absolute dilution. As an example, one of our graduate students once said that the sound of his boss's shoes in the morning office terrorized him because he feared the tasks he was about to receive! (To be fair we are pretty horrible bosses.) If you think the recent overuse of the term to absolute ridiculousness is a new phenomenon, almost 35 years ago in 1978, Laqueur wrote of,

If people were overusing the term in the 1970s, an era of hijackings and political extremists, why haven't we learned from them? *This vagueness as to what terrorism really is still holds in today's environment*. To understand just how varied these definitions are, we only have to look to the kaleidoscope of definitions of terrorism that occur just inside the United States.

First, let's state with U.S. law, Title 22 of the US Code, Section 2656f(d):

The most interesting limitation of this definition is the victim pool—they must be **noncombatants**. Given this definition the bombing of the Marine barracks in 1983 by the group Islamic Jihad would no longer be classified as a terrorist event. The limitation

> 66 *. . . the vagueness—indeed the utter carelessness—with which the term is used, not only in the media but also in government announcements and by academic students of the subject. Terrorism is used as a synonym for rebellion, street battles, civil strife, insurrection, rural guerrilla war, coup d'état, and a dozen other things. The indiscriminate use of the term not only inflates statistics, it makes understanding the specific character of terrorism and how to cope with it more difficult.* 99

> 66 *Terrorism is premeditated, politically motivated violence perpetrated against noncombatant targets by subnational groups or clandestine agents.* 99

of this definition also means that we can could no longer call attacks on U.S. soldiers abroad "terrorism" if they were committed by politically motivated groups.

The law goes on to say that international terrorism is "terrorism involving citizens or the territory of more than one country." This is a very narrow definition of international terrorism, especially in this melting pot of a country. All that is required to meet this definition is one participant in a terrorist event who is not a U.S. citizen. There is a case of domestic terrorism in the poisoning of a salad bar by the Rajneeshee religious cult in Oregon in 1984 to influence a local election. The full list of participants in this event is not clear, but if even one of them were to have a green card or be a "resident alien," this act would have been defined under U.S. law as international terrorism.

The U.S. Department of Defense (DoD), parent organization of all military forces, has its own definition of what constitutes terrorism. The DoD defines terrorism as

> " *The calculated use of unlawful violence or threat of unlawful violence to inculcate fear; intended to coerce or to intimidate governments or societies in the pursuit of goals that are generally political, religious, or ideological.* "

> " *... the unlawful use of force and violence against persons or property to intimidate or coerce a government, the civilian population, or any segment thereof, in furtherance of political or social objectives. (28 CFR Section 0.85)* "

The DoD definition focuses on *fear* and *coercion* and looks at the goals of the event, ignoring completely the type of victim as a determinant to what constitutes terrorism.

But wait, it doesn't stop there. The Federal Bureau of Investigation (FBI), whose mission is domestic federal law enforcement, further defines terrorism as

The FBI definition adds the previously unmentioned and specific term of *property*. While the presence of property damage might have been implied in other definitions, the FBI's inclusion of violence against property changes an event like intentionally burning a house from criminal to terrorism. This inclusion has significant impacts. By including crimes against property, the Earth Liberation Front (ELF) moves to the top of the FBI list of domestic terrorist groups prior to 9/11.

What is also interesting is the FBI, whose mission is solely domestic, feels the need to further define international terrorism:

> " *International terrorism involves violent acts or acts dangerous to human life that are a violation of the criminal laws of the United States or any state, or that would be a criminal violation if committed within the jurisdiction of the United States or any state. These acts appear to be intended to intimidate or coerce a civilian population, influence the policy of a government by intimidation or coercion, or affect the conduct of a government by assassination or kidnapping. International terrorist acts occur outside the United States or transcend national boundaries in terms of the means by which they are accomplished, the persons they appear intended to coerce or intimidate, or the locale in which their perpetrators operate or seek asylum. (FBI, 2012)* "

What is fascinating about the above definition is the transference of what would be illegal in this country to what is occurring in other countries. The FBI, which has no international jurisdiction or authority, *says act of violence* or *acts dangerous to human life* that occur outside this country are terrorism if they *would be a criminal violation if committed within the jurisdiction of the United States.*

What is also fascinating about the FBI's definition of international terrorism is the presence of the terms *assassination* and *kidnapping*. Assassinations are rarely included in definitions of terrorism because they are specific acts committed by a variety of people for a variety of reasons. Terror definitions don't usually include such specific acts is because these terms create difficult limitations. For example, when

President Reagan was shot by John Hinckley, Jr. because of Hinckley's obsession over the actress Jodi Foster, this can clearly be defined as an assassination attempt. Reagan lived, but had the president died, his assignation by the mentally unstable Hinckley would have been terrorism under the current FBI definition. (To really make things complicated what if Hinckley had been a "Resident Alien" from Honduras—would this now have been a case of international terrorism?)

The inclusion of the term *kidnapping* in the FBI's definition is also interesting. Most kidnappings are done for financial gain, with the expectation of a ransom to be paid out in exchange for the kidnapping victim. The most famous kidnapping in domestic history is the 1932 abduction of the 20-month-old Lindbergh baby, who was taken from his famous and wealthy parents. A ransom payment of $50,000 was paid for the baby's safe return, but unfortunately the baby died and was never reunited with his parents. As you can imagine, while this event was domestically important, it is by no means a terrorist act and is clearly for-profit criminal enterprise.

The core of defining terrorism is to be able to have a common language, to agree universally what terrorism is, and maybe someday have international laws that could persecute suspected terrorists.

Commonalities in Definitions of Terrorism

In order to assess the gap in definitions, the researchers Schmid and Jongman identified several commonalities in existing definitions. The following *recurring elements* were present in the 109 global definitions they assessed (Schmid & Jongman, 2005) :

- Violence or force: 83.5% of the definitions
- Political: 65%
- Fear, emphasis on terror: 51%
- Threats: 47%
- Psychological effect and anticipated reactions: 41.5%
- Discrepancy between the targets and the victims: 37.5%
- Intentional, planned, systematic, organized action: 32%
- Methods of combat, strategy, tactics: 30.5%

The question of violence is present in all definitions of terrorism, but it is not necessarily violence toward humans, but what is implied but never stated is violence as a crime. It is interesting to note that some definitions do not even allude to a crime or any illegality.

It is possible the only underlying characteristic within definitions is the use of violence or force. Gibbs writes, "Why do terrorists—state or nonstate—resort to secretive, furtive, and/or clandestine violence? *Because they seek goals that they perceive as realizable only through such violence* or only through legal means that entail unacceptable losses" (Gibbs, 1989). This ties back to Robespierre's thinking that *"Terror is nothing other than justice"* and can serve as a tool of statecraft.

What about "Legitimate Violence" or War?

The question of legitimate violence contributes to our understanding of terrorism. A commonly held distinction defines force employed by a state as legitimate, while the violence employed by a non-state actor is not legitimate. This distinction is the foundation of the difference between terrorism and war. War, which is declared and known by all parties involved, utilizes violence or the threat of violence by state actors, usually soldiers. However, actions that might be considered legitimate political violence in one jurisdiction may be considered criminal in another. This phenomenon occurs when soldiers from an outside country (legitimate political actors) behave in a way that citizens of the host country define as criminal or terrorism (i.e., targeting non-combatants or vital infrastructure).

The famous war theoretician Carl von Clausewitz (1832/1984) stated that war is comprised of "primordial violence, hatred, and enmity, which are to be regarded as blind, natural force." While Clausewitz meant this to apply to traditional warfare—two large state forces engaged on a battlefield—warfare is rarely conducted in this manner anymore, and his description now fits non-state actors just as well as state actors!

Countries that have experienced revolutionary conflict see political violence in a different light. In the distinction between war and terrorism, the historical high ground does little to define what could be a legitimate struggle. In a revolution, where citizens attempt to overthrow their existing government of societal system, the first actions of violence taken in the name of a revolution may be perceived as terrorism. It is the result of the revolution that defines the participants. If the revolutionaries win, they become state heroes. If the revolutionaries lose, they are defined as political dissidents or terrorists.

When the United Nations attempted to create a definition of terrorism in 2006, it wanted to include of any acts intended "to cause death or serious bodily harm to civilians." Some countries took exception to this proposition, raising the questions of whether the presence of a political agenda as the terrorist motive is necessary. This argument against killing civilians could reflect the motivation to eradicate an objectionable group of people, which is often based on an exclusivist religious rationale.

The legitimacy of political violence is also questioned in cases where citizens are resisting foreign occupation. The United Nations recognizes the problems faced by citizens who fight foreign occupiers but emphasize that no cause, no matter how just, can excuse terrorism.

What about Genocide? Is that Terrorism?

To further complicate the relationship between states, causes, and violence, there is the act of ethnic cleansing or genocidal violence. If the goal of violence is strictly exterminating a group of people perceived as undesirable—referred to euphemistically as "ethnic cleansing" by the perpetrators and as *genocide* by objective observers—then these actions could be possibly labeled as state-sponsored terrorism.

In the past, political motives have been claimed to provide an element of legitimacy to genocide (i.e., if we exterminate this group of people, there will be more resources for the rest of us); however, in reality genocides are rooted in hatred and xenophobia. This additional nomenclature in an already crowded field does little service to the core definition of terrorism and possibly even detracts from the concept of genocide.

The Role of Innocents

The presence of innocents, and the roles in terrorist acts, has often created the distinction between a terrorist act and other events. Binyamin Netanyahu introduced this concept in his definition of terrorism stating that terrorism is ". . . the deliberate and systematic murder, maiming, and menacing of the innocent to inspire fear for political ends" (Netanyahu, Terrorism; How the west can win, 1986). In his later works Netanyahu replaced the word "innocents" with "civilians" reworking his definition to state, "Terrorism is the deliberate and systematic assault on civilians to inspire fear for political ends" (Netanyahu, Fighting Terrorism, 1995). The Uniting Against Terrorism report also reiterates this message of innocents, claiming that no action, even a struggle for self-determination, allows for the deliberate killing or maiming civilians and non-combatants (Secretary-General of the UN Kofi Annan, 2006).

What if there is No Such Thing as Terrorism?

Ultimately it is important than any global definition would apply to all countries and would be one that both the adherents and abhorrers of terrorism could agree upon. But what if a single definition cannot exists because there is no such thing as terrorism anymore? What if everything we think of as terrorism can be parsed into the category of *warfare* or *criminal acts*? Within the category of *warfare* there is *asymmetrical warfare*, where forces that are vastly outnumbered use nontraditional means to engage and impact their enemy.

Now consider famous events we label as terrorism—in recent history we have the 1995 Oklahoma City bombing, which destroyed the Murrah Federal Building, killing 168, including 19 children in a daycare facility. The motivation for the Murrah building attack was retaliation for botched federal raids on Ruby Ridge and Waco. There is no denying this was an act of extraordinary violence, but with revenge as a motivation, is it still terrorism?

These examples are not mean to offend or upset the reader, but are intended to emphasize the subjective nature of the term *terrorism*.

The truth is, without an agreed upon definition of what terrorism is, we are without a common understanding. The key to this chapter is not to emphasize what is missing, but to provide you with an understanding of what is available so you can draw your own informed conclusions. As you create these conclusions, you will have the tools and theories to defend your ideas and continue an informed conversation.

Before the American Revolution began, a small group of men calling themselves the *"Sons of Liberty"* took to burning effigies and damaging or destroying homes of officials participating in the 1765 Stamp Act. The members of the Sons of Liberty group clearly fit our understanding of a terrorist group. Members were non-state actors whose goal was to subvert the government and incite change, using extraordinary violence and the destruction of property. Utilizing asymmetrical tactics, they operated in secret and threatened additional violence. The Boston Tea Party and other acts undertaken by the Sons of Liberty ultimately enhanced the conflict between the colonial government and the citizens, eventually culminating in the American Revolution.

"Boston Tea Party"

© Pete Spiro, 2013. Used under license from Shutterstock, Inc.

Now consider this, what if it had never become an official war? Are the acts of violence that could be considered terrorism redefined or negated if a war is declared? What is the difference between a *revolutionary* and a *terrorist*?

Ruby Ridge is the 1992 confrontation between the Weaver family and the FBI, U.S. Marshall Service, and the ATF resulting in the killing by the federal government of Weaver's wife and son. Waco was another fiasco resulting in a standoff for 50 days between several law enforcement agencies and a religious group of Branch Davidians. The standoff ended badly with a fire resulting from a federal assault that left 67 Branch Davidians dead, many of them women and children.

Key Terms

Psychological traits	Noncombatants
Extraordinary violence	Virtue
Moral aspects of terrorism	United Nations

Discussion Questions

1. If extraordinary violence is the only commonality in terrorism, can we use it as the foundation of a definition? Why? Why not?
2. What aspects should be included in a definition of terrorism?
3. Could there ever be a universal definition of terrorism, like there is for war? Why? Why not?

References

xAnnan, K. (2006). *Uniting against terrorism: Recommendations for a global.* New York: United Nations General Assembly.

Bonante, L. (1979). Some unintended consequences of terrorism. *Journal of Peace Research , 16*, 197–213.

Forst, B. (2009). *Terrorism, crime, and public policy.* Cambridge, England: Cambridge University Press.

Ganor, B. (2002). Defining terrorism: Is one man's terrorist another man's freedom fighter? (Routledge, Ed.) *Police Practice and Research, 3* (4), 287–304.

Laqueur, W. (1999). *The new Terrorism.* Oxford University Press.

Martin, G. (2013). *Understanding terrorism.* Thousand Oaks, CA: Sage.

Reich, R. (1998). *Origins of terrorism: Psychologies, ideologies, theologies, states of mind.* Washington, DC: Woodrow Wilson Center Press.

Schmid, A. P. (1983). *Political terrorism: A research guide to concepts, theories, data bases and literature.* New Brunswick, NJ: Transaction Publishers.

United Nations General Assembly GA/L/3433. (2012, October 8). Legal committee urges conclusion of draft comprehensive convention on international terrorism. *Sixty-seventh General Assembly, Sixth Committee, 1st & 2nd Meetings.* New York: UN Department of Public Information.

UShistory.org. (2012, December 19). *The Sons of Liberty.* Retrieved from www.ushistory. org/declaration/related/sons.htm

von Clausewitz, C. (1832/1984). *On war, indexed edition.* Princeton, NJ: Princeton University Press.

Wu, X. (2006, December 13). Kofi Annan's legacy on counterterrorism. *Harvard Center for Public Leadership News*, pp. Op-Ed.

Chapter 2

Why Terrorism Exists

Terrorism is not a new phenomenon, it will not vanish during our lifetime, and this sentiment is expressed in just about every textbook and article on the subject. The fact is, terrorism exists because of a perception that it can be effective in creating change. Think about all terrorist organizations throughout history; they all wanted something. They wanted to change a societal or cultural parameter, and for a variety of reasons they chose terrorism as a tool to effect that change. The question is not *what* they wanted changed, but *why* they used terrorism.

The central question to terrorism studies is, Why does terrorism exist at all? If we can answer that question, we can begin to design strategies and policies to prevent the formation of terrorist groups in the first place. That said, if this question was easily answered or addressed, there would be little need for the study of terrorism—we would already know all of the solutions.

Paths to Terrorism

A person does not wake up one morning, fix himself a cup of coffee, and spontaneously decide to carry out a terrorist attack. There is a path that led that person from to the point where he decides violence is the appropriate action to propagate change. This process of change and indoctrination, during which a person comes to believe that extremist and/or terrorist views and actions are accurate and appropriate, is called **radicalization**. The paths to radicalization are varied, but can be partially explained using three components: *rational choices*, **psychological models**, and *cultural and organizational influences.*

The path of each violent extremist or terrorist is different and may include features from any of these component parts. Additionally, single events or circumstances can have critical impacts on the radicalization of an individual. These **punctuated events** can create an atmosphere within a person or community that simplifies or accelerates radicalization.

Rational Choice Model

The **rational choice model** is not specific to the study of terrorism. In economics, the model illustrates that humans act in ways that are beneficial to them—they work toward their own self-interests. This is an easy concept to understand, and it

is easily illustrated in a variety of ways. If you are a student, you choose to attend a university because it will be beneficial to you in the future (remember, this an academic theory—don't bank on them all being true). You choose to forgo other opportunities (such as starting a career) as well as spend resources (time and money) on a degree because, from your point of view, it is in your best self-interest. The reverse is also true, rational choice also means we don't unusually undertake deliberately harmful courses of action that would be detrimental to our well-being.

It is easy to see a terrorist—a person who would perpetrate a violent attack against a civilian target—as "crazy," "deranged," or mentally unstable. This description gives us a mental health escape hatch; our failure to understand these actions can be simply writing them off as the work of insane people. Unfortunately, this easy out is also incorrect, and terrorists seldom suffer from mental illness. In fact, Marc Sageman, a researcher who interviewed and reviewed the biographies of over 170 terrorists, found that in his sample, the rate of mental illness was lower than the rate found in the general world population. In other words, terrorists are not clinically insane, at least not in greater frequency than the population of this university (or any community you are part of . . .).

Given the rational choice theory and the no mental health deficits, how do we explain the tendency or ability of some to blow up busses, hijack airplanes, kill hostages, or blow themselves up with suicide vests? The answer lies in how we define *self-interest*. Have you ever volunteered for a nonprofit organization, or a school, a library, or for a political campaign? Perhaps you served food to the homeless, collected canned goods, or helped prepare a Thanksgiving dinner for a battered women's shelter. You were probably not paid for that work—that is the definition of volunteering. Each of the activities costs you resources, and you got little or nothing in return. However, did those actions benefit you in some way? Not materially; in fact, they cost you something. You utilized your resources to volunteer; you gave time, gas money, and material items. You did this for little in the way of material returns. In the cold eyes of resource management, you came away with fewer resources than you started with. Your volunteering efforts were a net loss.

Does that mean that all of these actions were useless? Despite the fact that you received no resource compensation, were you, as a volunteer, working in your own self-interest? Of course you were. Resources aside, the rational choice model applies to intangible rewards as well. In our example, you felt "good" about what you were doing. You weighed the options and chose to give resources in exchange for something you believe in. You received intangible rewards for your resource contribution, and you felt the reward was worth the cost.

Terrorists make the same judgment. They are rational actors and have their own self-interests. Obviously, they are using a different set of values, but the reality is they exchange their limited resources for the reward of furthering their cause. Granted, you would (probably) not make the same choices, but they are working on a different moral frame than you are. Their moral beliefs, value systems, and their frame of reference is different from our point of view, allowing them to make decisions we would find repugnant.

The evidence supporting rational choice on the part of terrorists goes even further. We can clearly see rational decision making when we look at how terrorists and terrorist organizations utilize their resources. Remember, everyone has limited resources—time, money, supplies, and personnel. When was the last time you read a news story about a terrorist blowing up a tree in an empty field? You probably never have. Why not? Because blowing up a tree would cost resources (time, explosives, transportation, planning efforts, etc.) but would yield nothing of value to the terrorist. No one would care if a tree was blown up, and it would not change the social conditions at all. It is a poor cost-benefit equation. The rational terrorist performs this type of cost-benefit analysis constantly in recruitment, weapons acquisition and selection, target selection, attack timing, and method of attack. The terrorist organization uses a rational decision process to maximize the impact of its operations and drive change in its surroundings or society.

A similar rational decision process is demonstrated as nations and organizations employ counterterrorism measures. If a target is hardened or made more difficult to attack (reducing the probability of a successful attack), then the target is changed to one with a greater chance of success. This is a rational decision and is present in all aspects of terrorism.

We cannot escape the fact that terrorists are rational actors, carrying out goal-based activities to achieve a specific outcome, there is nothing "crazy" about them. However, do not confuse "rational" with "moral" or even "correct." Rationality only means the rational terrorist is acting in his or her own, or the organization's self-interest.

Psychological Models and Factors

It is difficult to understand how a mentally healthy person chooses to embrace violence and become or support a terrorist. The choice to carry out violent attacks against innocent or uninvolved citizens is incomprehensible to most of us. Psychologists have investigated this radicalization process for decades, and some models have emerged from the field that can be used to help us understand terrorism.

Early research into the psychological motivations of terrorists focused on terrorism as a *syndrome*. In other words, the terrorist was thought to be suffering from a psychological condition that could be explained through exploration of the situation and conditions surrounding the terrorist. The syndrome models are based on discovering the "root cause" of terrorism; factors such as poverty, political impotence, lack of education, declining Gross National Product.

Syndrome models imply that when a given individual is exposed to the various root causes, they can evolve into terrorists. The models fail to address why so few people (relatively) actually turn to violent extremism and terrorism to bring about social change. While we can gather empirical evidence about the external conditions that affect a person, it is difficult to research and measure internal factors and motivations that explain why one person reacts differently to the same set of external stimuli. In other words, why do some people become terrorists and some do not?

Staircase to Terrorism

One of the modern psychological theories of terrorism is the **Staircase to Terrorism model** developed by Fathali Moghaddam (2005). The Staircase Model describes the psychological process that leads to terrorism using the metaphor of climbing a staircase. An individual person begins on the ground floor, and through various conditions and decisions climbs upward, with each incremental step taking the person closer to terrorism. This type of decision making, though only having a single path, has proven useful in explaining behavior along a rational choice path.

The ground floor of the Staircase Model is where many of us reside. On the ground floor individuals focus on material conditions and self-improvements within society. If a person experiences **relative deprivation**—loss or perceived loss *that is disproportionate to the rest of society*—overall dissatisfaction may lead the person to proceed to the first floor. The relative aspect of the perceived deprivation is important, it allows even those who are very poor to differentiate themselves from the rest of their social strata or peers. Someone who lives in absolute poverty but is maintaining his or her livelihood and has flat or positive prospects for the future may not feel deprived; he or she is as well off as anyone else in his or her social circle. However, someone with expectations or threat of losing what little he has is suffering from relative deprivation. When looking at contributing factors of terrorism, it is almost always relative deprivation that becomes a driver of extremist behavior.

The first floor of the Staircase Model, or the second step, revolves around attempts at social mobility. Driven by the perceived unfair conditions and relative deprivation, the person on this floor is seeking solutions and opportunities to correct the injustice. If opportunities for legitimate (non-extremist) improvement and correction of the perceived loss are available, that may end the climb of the Staircase.

The second floor, or the third step, involves the potential terrorist learning to displace his anger or aggression. Once a person has learned to displace his aggression and dissatisfaction, and he seeks out opportunities to act on his aggression, he is ready to advance to the next step.

Moghaddam uses Freud's theories of displaced aggression to demonstrate how anti-American sentiment in the Middle East is actually the populace's anger at their own governments redirected to the United States. An example of displaced anger could include blaming your employer because your utilities were shut off. In this example, your employer failing to pay you allows you to project your irritation at not being able to afford your utility bill onto the perceived source of the problem.

The third floor in the Staircase Model introduces a would-be terrorist to an actual terrorist group. Through the concept of **moral engagement,** the new recruit aligns himself with the moral beliefs of the terrorist organization. Morale engagement allows an organization to recruit and indoctrinate potential terrorists and subverts individuals' belief systems to align with the moral framework of the organization. Terror organizational belief systems (moral framework) are not reflective of the morals found in general society. To convince the recruits they belong in the terror organization, moral engagement involves instilling a belief that perceived injustices (suffered during previous steps of the staircase) are from a shared enemy.

New members of an organization can be persuaded into the organization's moral framework through a variety of methods, and the reworking of our values and norms is called **cognitive reconstrual**. During cognitive reconstrual, the morals of an individual are changed. This usually includes dehumanizing any human targets, creating a psychological bridge that makes killing easier. Methods of moral disengagement and cognitive reconstrual typically include isolation from previous contacts, immersion into the new belief system, and the creation of fear and distrust of others. These methods allow the terrorist organization to subvert existing moral systems and replace them with its own. The illegal, secretive, and threatened nature of the terrorist organization is a powerful amplifier of these effects. Once a new recruit is immersed into the terrorist organization, he feels the "persecution" of the new organization (by outsiders or government), and this feeds his shift in moral frameworks, making the overall moral engagement easier.

On the fourth floor, the person has fully entered the terrorist organization and is developing skills and abilities to further the goals of the group. His or her immersion in a small, selective, and secret organization serves to add legitimacy to goals and further aligns the recruit with the organizational desires. The new terrorist is trained or given specific abilities and specializations to support the organization, which further completes his or her immersion and indoctrination. Once this indoctrination is complete, attempting to leave the group or move back down the staircase is no longer possible. The fourth floor of the Staircase Model cements the "us versus them" mindset and prepares individuals for the fifth and final floor.

The fifth (and final) floor prepares the terrorist to carry out an attack that will kill or cause injury. It is at this time that the terrorist is trained to kill or use a variety of violent methods. By expanding on the previous moral engagement, the target is branded as an outsider or "them". The combination of dehumanizing targets, identifying them as other or outsiders, and associating them with a threat against the organization paints a clear picture of the enemy. This entire process builds on the new moral framework adopted on the third floor and allows the terrorist to sidestep moral mechanisms that typically prevent extraordinary violence and murder. Terrorists who have reached the fifth floor of the Staircase Model are motivated, trained, morally prepared, supported by an entire organization, and obviously very dangerous.

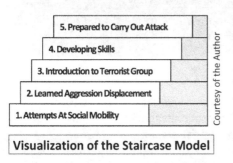

5. Prepared to Carry Out Attack
4. Developing Skills
3. Introduction to Terrorist Group
2. Learned Aggression Displacement
1. Attempts At Social Mobility

Courtesy of the Author

Visualization of the Staircase Model

The Staircase Model is designed as an explanatory framework—a tool to help us understand the progression of the person to extremism and terrorism. The Staircase model was designed after examining specifically Islamic extremists and terrorists, but other researchers have validated parts of the model against other types of terrorists and terrorist organizations.

However, there are problems with this model, notably the implication that progression on the Staircase is predetermined—that given the set of conditions and behaviors defined on each step, the person will progress to the next step. This may not always be the case, the path of radicalization is varied, and potential terrorists may move up or down on the staircase, possibly never reaching the next step or carrying out a terrorist attack. Further, the model does not allow for a person to skip a step, implying that every terrorist will experience all phases of the model. The Staircase Model also fails to address an individual who creates the organization and may have been the originator, or those in leadership positions. These variations in how a person progresses in the model is true for any such construct; there is not a single defined path to terrorism.

Terrorism as a Tool

Other psychological research into terrorism and its roots looks at *terrorism as a tool*, rather than a syndrome or condition. This approach minimizes the attempts to identify the root causes of terrorism and instead looks at terrorist attacks as a weapon or a technique. Like Robespierre suggested, a person or organization can employ terrorism the same way an individual or government uses violent methods to further its goal. In this approach, the definition of *terrorist* is not rooted in a psychological conditions predicated by environmental factors, but is simplified to mean a *person who employs terrorism as a tactic*.

Just because we are minimizing the importance of "root causes" of terrorism does not mean we can eliminate these factors from consideration. Conditions that provide root cause (poverty, personal grievances, perceived injustices, political environment, etc.) are still critical to our understanding, but they are reduced to the level of contributing factors.

The terrorism as a tool approach does a better job of explaining how one person, in a given society, and pressured by the same factors, can choose terrorism while 50 others do not. Further, the terrorism as a tool approach suggests that any actor could become a terrorist by employing the tool of a terrorist attack. With a wide range of terrorist organizations and goals, and lacking a single "terrorist profile," the terrorism as a tool concept fits the global conditions we face today.

We live in the information age. You could, in the next 30 minutes (probably less), download detailed information on how to carry out an effective terrorist attack. Al Qaeda publishes a quarterly glossy magazine (on the Internet) that will teach you to build a bomb, care for your rifle, and travel without raising suspicion. The simple availability of information on how to conduct a terrorist attack lends weight to the terrorism as a tool argument; anyone can employ any number of violent tactics to further his or her ideological or political goals. However, should the use of the tactics automatically make you a terrorist? If a single gunman shoots his fellow students in a classroom, should the gunman be labeled a terrorist?

There is a tendency in the United States to view our current era as "The Global War on Terrorism" or GWOT. This concept or definition conveys a sense that the United States is in a struggle with a single enemy, a global organization, or at least a group of like-minded individuals. However, when we apply the terrorism as tool concept, the GWOT argument of an identifiable enemy loses its relevance. It becomes the equivalent of a War on Rifles (go easy on your Second Amendment rants, we're not advocating taking away gun rights in the United States) or a War on Assassination or a War on Bank Robbery. These things may be something we want to eradicate, but it's not something a nation declares war on.

A Tool of Coercion

Thomas Schelling (1966) wrote that military force can be used to inflict "hurt" on an enemy, and the fear of that hurt can motivate the opponent to avoid it. This coercive action, forcing an opponent to change policy or direction by threatening violence against them, is a cornerstone of terrorism as a tool. Schelling's arguments were aimed primarily at diplomacy and conflict of nations and states, but they are applied as easily to non-state actors and terrorists. "The power to hurt is bargaining power. To exploit it is diplomacy—**vicious diplomacy**, but diplomacy" (Schelling, 1966). When an organization employs terrorism, it is displaying "vicious" diplomatic power; it is using coercion as a tactic.

The issue is that terrorism as a tool removes terrorism as something we are fighting, and requires us to better define our enemy. In our current era, from a Western or U.S. perspective, we may see the enemy as a loose network of Islamic extremist organizations that target Western interests. In previous eras, the enemy may have been defined as dissident political groups or separatists or anarchists. Each of these types of terrorist organizations employed terrorism as a tool, but for very different reasons. In an effort to be effective we must focus on these contributing factors, as well as the goals of the organization, and work to counter them.

Cultural and Organizational Influence

No one lives in an isolated vacuum; we are influenced by family, friends, co-workers, classmates, and countless others. Our media-rich culture extends influence across the world almost instantaneously, and our communications reach is limited only by imagination. Extremists and terrorists live in the same conditions.

Martha Crenshaw (1981) wrote that terrorism is a group activity, involving intimate relationships among a small number of people. The presence of the group identity is of upmost importance when attempting to understand the disposition of the individual. Researchers for decades have understood the importance of the group dynamic on the development and behavior of the individual terrorist. Most psychological studies of terrorism depend on the extraordinary influence of the terrorist group, combined with the perceived injustice and dissatisfaction of the potential terrorist to explain the acceptance of a violent moral frame and the resulting willingness to kill.

The relationship between the individual and the group builds trust and solidarity among the terrorists and reinforces the organization's belief system. Ultimately, strengthening this group cohesion is the individual terrorist's adherence to that system. The terrorist group becomes the only source of safety and respite for the terrorist, and this support system is critical to the ongoing participation of the individual.

Punctuated Events

There is occasionally a single event or chain of events that drives a person or group towards terrorism. These *punctuated events* are high profile and notable, and examples include bombings, government crackdowns, or sudden elimination or reduction of rights and privileges. When these types of events occur, they can add to the distrust or dissatisfaction of the population and may foster activity to counter the event. For example, the Ruby Ridge and Waco events were considered punctuated events in law enforcement history and served to motivate McVeigh and Nichols to retaliate by bombing the Murrah Federal Building in Oklahoma City.

Countering these punctuated events may include peaceful and legal activities such as protests, rallies, petitions, or political campaigns, but they can also include violence and terrorism. The choice of counter activities will be influenced by where on the path to terrorism a person is, as well as the cultural or moral frame the person employs. Sudden crackdowns against dissident groups may accelerate the moral engagement process—and help foster and create terrorism.

We cannot ignore the fact that terrorist attacks and other violent events are often themselves punctuated events that drive change. In the case of these events, the punctuated events seldom foster additional terrorism but instead drive policy and societal changes to counter the threat of terrorism. Examples in the United States include the legislative and administrative changes in the federal government in response to the September 11, 2001 attacks. These changes were designed by lawmakers and administrators to increase the security and safety of the United States, but included actions and policy that would not have existed without the stimulus of the 9/11 attacks.

Punctuated events are profoundly influenced by media coverage. We will delve deeper in the media effects on terrorism later in this book, and it must be noted that in many ways the media contributes to the conflagration of punctuated events. While these landmark events are critical in driving public policy decisions, and they may foster or encourage extremism and terrorism, they also bring acknowledgement or notoriety to the perpetrators of the attack, and those who report and cover the stories.

Morality and Terrorism

Defining an event as terrorism, or a person as a terrorist, is often a function of perspective. The classic saying, "One man's terrorist is another man's freedom fighter" illustrates this point. While the actions of a person or group may be classified from one perspective as terrorism; from the opposite view, those same people or actions may appear to be heroic or in defense of society or community. In other words, how do we distinguish terrorism from "legitimate" political violence? We would expect this ambiguity to continue when we look in detail at the justifications of terrorism, but that is seldom the case. We must resist the urge to brand terrorists as "crazy" or "irrational" because they choose to employ violence in a way that is unjustified or immoral. We view these events through our moral frame, but the societal morality is different from the terrorists. Remember that as a person progresses on the path to terrorism, he or she undergoes a shift in moral views that allows violence directed toward the "other" or the oppressors.

Terrorism involves extraordinary violence resulting in injury, death, or the destruction of property. However, this violence differs from that associated with criminal acts or "simple" murder. What is this distinction and can we define terrorism in such a way to make that distinction clear? (See Chapter 1.) In practice, deaths from terrorist attacks are murder, but they are also something more.

The previous examples show that our society has many conditions on which killing is justifiable according to the laws governing the people. These acts may be distasteful, but they are commonly not defined as murder. Using the **moral frame** familiar to most Americans, killing in self-defense is justifiable while preemptively attacking and killing innocent civilians is not. How do we, morally, separate terrorism from murder? How do we separate terrorism from justified killing? How do we separate terrorism from warfare?

In general, there are three factors that help us differentiate and identify terrorism from the above examples: *(1) who the attackers are, (2) who they are attacking,* and *(3) the intent of the attackers*. Not all factors apply to all terrorist activities and attacks, but these assist us in determining the morality of the attack.

1. *Terrorism is perpetrated by individuals or non-state groups*. There is some gray area here, as some states do sponsor and support terrorism, and this is discussed more in Chapter 3. If the attack or violence is coming from a state military, it is difficult to classify this as terrorism. In general, terrorists are usually not conscripts, soldiers, or people who are ignorant of the causes

If a man breaks into a home, and the homeowner shoots and kills the intruder with a firearm, is that murder? In most U.S. jurisdictions, the answer is no. If a man is attacked on the street and defends himself, and in the ensuing struggle the attacker is killed, is that murder? Again, in most U.S. jurisdictions the answer would be no. When a military force conducts combat operations, the intent is to kill or disable enemy forces, is this murder? Under generally accepted international convention, the answer is no. If a military force engaged in legally directed combat operations accidently kills civilians, is that murder? These cases of "collateral damage" occur in military combat operations in every theater of war. They are seldom classified as war crimes or murder unless the military commander or forces are deemed to have been negligent or operating illegally. Again, no on murder.

driving their actions. They are not ignorant pawns; they were not forced or coerced into action; they are aware and complicit.

2. *Terrorism is directed at innocent bystanders.* Innocent in this context describes the person's noninvolvement in the dispute or conflict; the victim is a bystander, usually a civilian. The apparently random nature of the attack lends to the creation of fear and terror. Depending on the situation, attacks on deployed or uniformed combatants are usually not classified as terrorism.

3. *Terror is the intent of the terrorism.* In our self-defense example, the intent was not to create terror but to protect life. Also, the criminal who broke into a home was most likely after personal gain, and terror was a secondary factor. Collateral damage will cause fear and terror in those that witness it, but that was not the intent of the attack.

These factors do not create a complete, foolproof moral compass for identifying terrorist attacks, but they provide a valuable moral framework for discerning possibly justifiable violence from terrorism. Given this framework, are there situations or instances of morally justifiable terrorism? If violence in self-defense is justifiable, can that same precept by applied to terrorism?

To answer these questions, we turn to the work of Saul Smilansky who explored several cases looking for examples of truly justifiable terrorism. Smilansky (2004) looked at the Irish Republican Army (IRA) in Northern Ireland and its struggle against the British government.

A citizen of Northern Ireland is also a citizen of the United Kingdom and as such enjoys the rights and protections entitled to all UK citizens. These include political rights and the freedom to practice any religion, as well as political representation and the benefits of a functional and supported local government. If the citizen found those protections unsuitable, he could easily move miles to the south and take up residence in the Republic of Ireland, which is not governed by the UK. The Republic of Ireland, which occupies five-sixths of all Ireland, is a free and open society, with protections for citizens, including cultural and religious freedom. A citizen of Northern Ireland is free to move to or associate with the Republic of Ireland.

The Irish Republican Army (IRA) was formed to eliminate British rule of Northern Ireland and unite the two Irelands, but the shape of the conflict took a religious tone with the IRA representing a Catholic Ireland and the British being associated with Protestant rule. Despite the rhetoric and statements of the IRA, the comparative conditions between Protestants and Catholics in Northern Ireland were not that severe. What relative deprivation Catholics living in Northern Ireland experienced was minor when compared to the struggles facing other cultures living in more oppressive societies. Once violent action was taken by the IRA against representatives or symbols of British rule, security measures imposed by the British government increased the relative deprivation, and many of these measures acted as punctuated events, further driving terrorist actions. The British reaction to IRA events created a self-fulfilling prophecy and terrorism became a self-perpetuating cycle.

Smilansky found that in places where terrorism may be justified (violence to protect a society or group against a repressive government or faction), it did not flourish. In places where terrorism flourished, it was not justified (including the IRA example from above). This leads us then to the conclusion that while terrorism may, in some cases, be a justifiable tool of the oppressed, examples of this in practice are rare or nonexistent. Maybe the "freedom fighter" quote is a misguided attempt to complicate the issue?

Why Terrorism Still Exists

If terrorism has been shown to be unjustified violence against innocent targets, why is it still employed? Simply, because it works. That may not be the answer you were looking for (or expecting), but the reality is that terrorism works. The catch to that statement is how we define "works."

Rarely do terrorist organizations completely achieve their stated goals through violence. However, terrorist attacks can succeed in changing society in a way that favors the terrorist organization's cause. Even if that was not the case, terrorism "works" in the sense that brings attention and support to the cause of the organization, even while the overall goal may remain out of reach.

Case Study: Madrid Train Bombing

On March 11, 2004, 10 explosive devices detonated on four commuter trains in and around Madrid, Spain. The explosions were timed within minutes of each other, and the coordinated attacks killed 191 people and wounded another 1,841.

All of the targeted trains had departed Alcalá de Henares Station located approximately 18 miles outside of Madrid. The four trains were filled with morning commuters, and the devices detonated as the trains were in or near stations. Three devices failed to detonate and were later disarmed; these devices provided valuable evidence toward identifying the attackers.

The Spanish government had been locked in conflict with the Basque separatist movement Euskadi Ta Askatasuna (ETA) for over 40 years. ETA was formed in 1959 with the goal of Basque regional autonomy in northern Spain, and included heavy Marxist ideology. Over the last half of the 20th century, the group had carried out kidnappings, robberies, and assassination until a ceasefire was declared in 1998. The ceasefire didn't last, and ETA renewed terrorist attacks in early 2000, resulting in a new wave of government crackdowns.

It is not surprising that the Spanish government almost immediately declared ETA responsible for the 2004 Madrid train bombing. The initial accusations, including public statements by senior government officials, declared there was "no doubt" that ETA was responsible. This conclusion and identification of an old enemy created a sense of national unity in Spain, much like what followed in the United States after the 9/11 attacks. Peaceful protests against violence were held the day after the attacks, and Spanish society was comfortable with blaming the longtime separatist enemy. However, in less than three days after the explosions, officials began looking at Islamic extremists with ties to al Qaeda. This shift in focus, led by the physical evidence in the unexploded devices, was unpopular with the Spanish leadership and the once-peaceful protests became anti-government and anti-Islamic mobs, as the people perceived their government as inept and corrupt.

At the time of the attack, Spain was an ally of the United States in the invasion of Iraq and Spanish troops were serving in the Gulf. This decision to back the United States was unpopular with Spaniards, with some polls showing a disapproval rating of almost 90%. After the train bombing, while public government statements continued to blame ETA, physical evidence provided links to Islamic extremists, and Spanish police were tracking down and arresting people with connections to al Qaeda. When these arrests of suspected bombers become known, the public erupted in anger—at both the attackers and the government. In further confirmation, an al Qaeda group in Europe released a videotape claiming responsibility for the attacks.

The group claiming responsibility for the bombings suggested they were retaliations for the continued Spanish military support of the United States in Iraq. The population quickly came to the conclusion that the attacks would not have occurred, and al Qaeda would not have targeted Spain if the Spanish government had not deployed troops to Iraq.

Three days after the explosions, Spanish national elections occurred. In the midst of public anger at the government and a growing certainty that Islamic terrorists were responsible for the latest horror, the Spanish Socialist Workers Party won a surprise upset victory against the incumbent administration. Three days after the elections, six days after the bombing, Spain had a new prime minister and a new government. A month after being elected, the new prime minister ordered all Spanish troops home. Spanish support for the U.S.-led coalition in Iraq was over.

Even a cursory review of the events and the aftermath shows an outcome that favors Islamic al Qaeda affiliates in Spain and Europe. The new Spanish government withdrew support for the war in Iraq and brought all Spanish troops home. Was this outcome a deliberate goal of the March 11 attacks, or were they a coincidence? Popular coverage in the United States and Europe claimed the Spanish electorate had "appeased" the terrorists by electing a party and government that would withdraw from Iraq. This appeasement claim implies success by al Qaeda and its affiliates. Unfortunately, the issue is not that clear.

The assumption by much of the world that al Qaeda affiliates responsible for the Madrid bombings were successful is based on the fact that a new government was elected three days after the attacks. This new government was less supportive of the U.S.-led war in Iraq, and subsequently withdrew Spanish troops. On the surface, it appears that the Madrid bombings were coercive in nature to the Spanish people because they voted to change the national policy that they believed led to the attacks. This agreement—to vote the way the attackers wanted in response to pain—appears to be coercive. As we discussed earlier in this chapter, this type of usage of terrorism—to change a governmental policy—is a type of vicious diplomacy. However, recent analysis of the Madrid attacks shows that a true coercive bargain may not exist in this case.

A coercive bargain has several key components. First, the terrorist must have the demonstrated ability to cause harm. It is clear that al Qaeda affiliates in Spain and Europe possessed that capability and demonstrated its use. Second, the coercive bargain implies that if the attacker's demands are met, the attacker will refrain from further attacks. In other words, if Spain agrees to the demands (withdrawal from Iraq and Afghanistan), further bombings will not occur. This restrictive ability (a willingness not to attack) has never been demonstrated by al Qaeda—and the Spanish would have no assurance that it would be true. Further, the demands included withdrawal from both Iraq and Afghanistan, and Spanish support did not waiver in Afghanistan. They viewed the invasion in 2001, and subsequent war there, to be just and correct. To sum this up, the Spanish people did not actually vote to meet terrorist demands, they voted for the party they felt was best positioned to meet the terrorist threat given the current circumstances. In general, this is an example of an action=reaction event, and not necessarily coercive.

Overall, the Madrid train bombings had a significant impact on Spanish politics, and that effect benefitted al Qaeda and its affiliates. The bombing also demonstrated al Qaeda's capability in Europe resulting in a recruiting and awareness boon. From that aspect, we still label the Madrid bombings as a successful terrorist attack, but it is not clear Spain was coerced into action.

In 2007 al Qaeda claimed to be proud of the attacks and the changes it wrought in Spain. Despite all the physical evidence, arrests, and subsequent convictions, those two claims are the extent of the direct links between the Madrid train bombing and al Qaeda affiliates. Many of the conspirators were linked to a variety of Islamic al Qaeda affiliate organization, and none were linked to ETA.

Key Terms

Cognitive reconstrual

Moral engagement

Moral frame

Psychological models

Punctuated event

Rational choice model

Radicalization

Relative deprivation

Staircase to Terrorism model

Vicious diplomacy

Discussion Questions

1. Should tactics used determine if you are a terrorist? Why? Why not?

2. What is the Global War on Terrorism?

3. What are some examples of groups and organizations that practice cognitive reconstrual and moral engagement, but are not terrorists?

References

Alderdice, J. (2009). Values, empathy, and fairness across social barriers. *Annals of the NY Academy of Sciences, 1167,* 158–173.

Anderton, C., & Carter, J. (2006). On rational choice theory and the study of terrorism. *Defence and Peace Economics, 16.4,* 275–282.

Caplan, B. (2005). Terrorism: The relevance of the rational choice model. *Public Choice, 128,* 91–107.

Corte, L. (2007). Explaining terrorism: A psychosocial approach. *Perspectives on Terrorism, 1.2*

xCrenshaw, M. (1981). The causes of terrorism. *Comparative Politics, 13.4,* 379–399.

Dannenbaum, T. (2011). Bombs, ballots, and coercion: The Madrid bombings, electoral politics, and terrorist strategy. *Security Studies, 20,* 303–349.

Davis, P., & Cragin, K. (Eds). (2009). *Social science of counterterrorism: Putting the pieces together*. Santa Monica, CA: The RAND Corporation

Ernst-Vintila, A., Delouvee, S., & Roland-Levy, C. (2011). Lay thinking about terrorism and the three-dimensional model of personal involvement: A social psychological analysis. *Journal of Risk Research, 14.3,* 297–324

Freedman, L. (2007). Terrorism as a strategy. *Government and Opposition*, 42.3, 314–339.

Kamm, F. (2006). Terrorism and several moral distinctions. *Legal Theory, 12,* 19–69.

Krieger, T., & Meierrieks, D. (2011). What causes terrorism? *Public Choice, 147.1-2,* 3–27

Kuznar, L., & Lutz, J. (2007). Risk sensitivity and terrorism. *Political Studies, 55,* 341–361.

Loza, W. (2007). The psychology of extremism and terrorism: A Middle-Eastern perspective. *Aggression and Violent Behavior, 12*, 141–155

Lygre, R., Eid, J., Larsson, G., & Ranstop, M. (2011). Terrorism as a process: A critical review of Moghaddam's "Staircase Terrorism." *Scandinavian Journal of Psychology, 52,* 609–616.

Kruglanski, A., & Fishman, S. (2007). The psychology of terrorism: "Syndrome" versus "tool" perspectives. *Terrorism and Political Violence, 18.2,* 193–215.

Kydd, A., & Walter, B. (2006). The strategies of terrorism. *International Security, 31.1,* 49–80.

Mazarr, M. (2004). The psychological sources of Islamic terrorism. *Policy Review, 125,* 39–60

xMoghaddam, F. (2005). The Staircase to Terrorism. *American Psychological Association, 60.2,* 161–169.

Post, J. (2010). When hatred is bred in the bone: The social psychology of terrorism. *Annals of the NY Academy of Sciences, 1208,* 15–23

Pyszczynski, T., Rothschild, Z., & Abdollahi, A. (2008). Terrorism, violence, and hope for peace. *Current Direction in Psychological Science, 17.5,* 318–322

Sageman, M. (2004). Understanding terror networks. Philadelphia: University of Pennsylvania Press.

Scheuer, J. (1990). Moral dimensions of terrorism. *Forum of World Affairs, 14*, 145–160.

xSchelling, T. (1966). *The diplomacy of violence, arms and influence*. New Haven: Yale University Press. At www.americaandtheworld.com/assets/media/pdfs/Schelling.pdf

Shughart, W. (2011). Terrorism in rational choice perspective. In C. Coyne & R. Mathers (Eds.), *Political economy of war* (pp. 126–153). Northampton, MA: Edward Elgar Publishing.

xSmilansky, S. (2004). Terrorism, justification, and illusion. *Ethics, 114.4,* 790–805.

Taylor, M. (2010). Is terrorism a group phenomenon? *Aggression and Violent Behavior, 15,* 121–129.

Zarakol, A. (2011). What makes terrorism modern? Terrorism, legitimacy, and the international system. *Review of International Studies, 37.5,* 2311–2336.

Chapter 3

Types of Terrorism

Now that you know the actors and understand the motivations of terrorism, you can begin to learn the different types of terrorism. As you understand these categories, it is important to recognize that groups may fall exclusively into one type of group, or they may be defined by multiple definitions. Usually when we identify a terrorist organization as "transnational" or "religious" it means that its primary motivation and purpose is best reflected by this description. In order to give you the tools to impress your friends and family, by the end of this chapter it will be easy for you to talk authoritatively on groups that might be "state-sponsored international religious dissidents."

Dissident or Vigilant Terrorism

Starting at the local level are homegrown terrorists, and like buying locally, these are terrorists who are native to and are using violence in their own country. As was mentioned in previous chapters, terrorists are always motivated by change, and despite their illegal actions, are rational in thought. **Domestic terrorists** are actors "from below" who commit terrorism against people in their own government or other groups within their country. These domestic actors may be vigilante groups that seek change through violent political action, and vigilantes will sometime target a specific type of person like a vegetarian, a Muslim, a Haitian, or a New Yorker. A common rallying point of dissidents and vigilantes in this country is **xenophobia**, which is a fear of outsiders. When combined with **nativism**, a belief in the superiority of one's own homeland, you get domestic hate groups.

Case Study: Ku Klux Klan

The litany of people the KKK identify as "other" and who they would like to live without is extensive and includes anyone not white, immigrants, non-Christians, and communists. Still active in the United States, with membership estimated between 3,000 and 5,000, KKK members traditionally meet in secret. When committing acts involving violence, members wear a white robe and pointed hood to disguise their identity. The group's adopted use of a disguise is a unique phenomenon in terrorism; the KKK outfit has been worn since the group's inception in the 1860s and is now symbolically recognizable as exclusive to the KKK. (Unless you are the Capirote in Spain, who wear similar outfits.)

© Stefano Penzari, 2013. Used under license from Shuttershock, Inc.

KKK Mask

Interestingly, xenophobic groups often target government officials or symbols because of U.S. policies regarding equality and integration. Nativist hate groups often reference actions by the U.S. government against white separatist groups, and one of the classic examples is federal actions in Waco and Ruby Ridge. For Timothy McVeigh and Terry Nichols, two young, white, former members of the U.S. Army, the motivation to attack the Oklahoma City Murrah Federal Building was in retaliation for the government's handling of the Waco and Ruby Ridge sieges.

In the case of vigilante or dissident terrorists, while the government may be the target, the terror group may have the support or acquaintance of government officials. Confused? Let's help that discussion with an example.

The anti-abortion or pro-life movement has made an effort to overturn legislation in the United States that allows legal abortions. Most of the anti-abortion movement has been peaceful and uses traditional political methodologies to change the law. However, there have been domestic terror groups, like the Army of God (AOG), that have used violence to draw attention to the anti-abortion cause. These groups, including the AOG, have committed clear domestic acts of terror: blowing up buildings, killing doctors and their families, and threatening politicians. While no government official supports this type of violence as an effort to change the abortion laws, some do support the desire to change or eliminate the law. This type of support is sometimes called "ideological support" when you agree with the idea but not the actions (see Chapter 4).

Ruby Ridge (August 1992)

Randy Weaver and his family lived in a small cabin in northern Idaho because of their strong distrust of the government and apocalyptic beliefs. Weaver had weak ties to the Aryan Nation and was being investigated by the ATF for allegedly selling illegal firearms to an informant. When he was approached to be an informant himself, he declined and was put on trial. His trial date was moved without his knowledge and he failed to show up in federal court, leading to a bench warrant for his arrest. The U.S. marshals made multiple attempts to get Weaver to surrender, but his distrust led to increasing levels of threats and surveillance as time moved forward. After a brief shoot-out in the middle of the night between Weaver's son and the U.S. Marshals (in which the son was killed), the cabin was surrounded and a nine-day siege began. During the siege Weaver was shot and injured and his wife was shot and killed. The remaining Weavers surrendered, and Randy Weaver was acquitted of all charges except failure to appear in court.

Waco Siege (February–April 1993)

David Koresh led a small sect of Christians, known as Branch Davidians, who lived on a small plot of land outside of Waco, TX. Koresh was suspected of engaging in polygamy, statutory rape, and child abuse, but was charged with hording illegal weaponry. An initial attempt to execute a search warrant resulted in a shoot-out that caused the death of four agents and six Branch Davidians. A 50-day siege commenced in which the FBI increasingly feared for the well-being of the children being held inside. The final day of the siege three fires of undetermined origin broke out in the complex. In the end 76 people, including some children, refused to leave and were trapped by the fires, resulting in their deaths.

Dissident Objectives and Targets

Dissident terrorists are attempting to change the political schema of their society. They may be separatists, looking for some level of autonomy ("We just want to be left to ourselves"), or they may want to see significant changes in the social fabric of society ("We don't like the fact that our government is left-leaning"). In most cases, dissidents have clear objectives—they can tell you why they want something, and they are using terrorism as a means to raise awareness for their cause. The Weather Underground Group in the United States is a good example. It carried out attacks in the 1960s and 1970s to force the United States to end the war in Vietnam. To that end, dissident terrorist groups often target symbols of the government or social structure they are opposing. The Irish Republican Army often targeted the British military or police stations. The Red Brigade in Italy was attempting to establish a Marxist society and remove Italy from the North Atlantic Treaty Organization and often targeted politicians for assassination and kidnapping—again, members struck at the symbols of what they opposed.

Sub-revolutionary Terrorism

There is a term sometimes used in terrorism studies called **sub-revolutionary terrorism** and this term can befuddle readers. In the same way you cannot be *a little bit pregnant,* you can't really be *a little bit revolutionary*. While it is possible that acts of terrorism become a movement leading to a revolution, this doesn't change the distinction between the two. Domestic dissident acts using violence or the threat of violence against a seated government in the name of change are terrorism. The presence of a manifesto, petition, or cause does not make a revolution; your movement becomes a revolution when citizens openly rally behind the cause (in the name of the cause). If the larger political status quo is maintained, then the revolution has failed. If a new political paradigm is instituted, then a revolution has succeeded. Once a country enters a revolution, there is usually only one type of outcome: Someone wins and someone loses. If the revolutionary movement wins, all the previous acts leading up to the revolution are identified in a "heroes' perspective." If the government wins and quashes the revolution, all the early dissidents keep their status as rabble-rouser terrorists.

People often ask what the difference is between dissident terrorism and a revolution, and part of the answer is in the eyes of the winner. If you look at a historic act like the Boston Tea Party, where property belonging to a seated government was destroyed to draw attention to a cause or movement, it is clearly terrorism. However, the Boston Tea Party is part of what led to the American Revolution, a clearly defined war between an active colonial government and citizens of that land. Since the starters of the revolution ended up being the winners of that conflict, we address the acts leading up to the revolution in a very different way than if we had lost. If the British had won the American Revolution, you can be assured that events such as the Boston Tea Party would be referred to as acts of aggression and terrorism by insurgents who were subsequently punished. (It's possible that's still how British textbooks read.)

State-Sponsored Terrorism

Often called "terrorism from above," **state-sponsored terrorism** is perpetrated by the government against its own people. Using terror tactics to enforce or conduct activities that might undermine the public or international trust, state-sponsored terror seeks to remove perceived enemies or unwanted groups. State-sponsored actions are hostile and violent and occur outside a declared war; they generally target civilians or individuals the state chooses not to deal with by legal means.

The actors who perpetrate this violence are often agents of the state and sometimes may be part of an existing government structure. They can act covertly and in some cases special insignia-wearing groups (or even the government's regular military) have conducted state-sponsored terrorism.

If a government does choose to use terror tactics against its own people, the covertness of the actions can allow the state to claim "**plausible deniability**" saying it didn't know what was occurring. An example of this can be found in Zimbabwe where civilian-attired death squads would routinely kill supporters of opponents to incumbent president Robert Mugabe. In power for 33 years through "free elections," Mugabe's death squads start targeting civilians well before election day, including any political opponents and their families, ensuring absolute fear in voting or speaking out against Mugabe.

An example of state-sponsored terrorism using the military can be found in the Halabja gas attacks in northern Iraq against the Kurdish minority. Ordered by the Iraqi government, the government dropped chemical weapons on a small Kurdish town north of Baghdad. To this day the gas compound used is unknown but is thought to a combination of mustard gas, VX, sarin, and tabun, and casualties are estimated between 7,000–8,000 Iraqi Kurds.

Within state sponsorship it is also important to distinguish between domestic and international focus. Because it is the government doing the terrorizing, usually covertly and without public fanfare regarding its actions, the state can direct actions at either its own citizens or internationally at citizens abroad. Both of the examples provided previously in Zimbabwe and Iraq were *state-sponsored domestic terror* events, but there are plenty of examples of *state-sponsored international terror.*

One of the most famous state-sponsored international terrorist organizations was the Palestinian Liberation Organization (PLO), whose identified enemies were Israel and the United States. (The PLO was officially taken off the State Department list of Foreign Terror Organizations (FTO) in 1991.) The PLO was founded in an effort to self-determine a homeland for the Palestinian people and was comfortable advocating violence against other countries to further the PLO cause. In a perfect example of state sponsorship, it was other organizations affiliated with the PLO—the PLFP, PPP, PLF, and others—that actually perpetrated the acts of terrorism on the behalf of the Palestinian movement. No one involved in international relations believed the PLO was uninvolved, but technically the PLO could point to these other organizations and say they were separate. Considered the worst kept secret in international affairs, the PLO used operational arms of the organization to set off bombs in Israel, to hijack international planes, and to famously hijack a cruise ship, the *Achillie Lauro,* where PLO affiliates shot and threw a wheel-chair-bound Jewish man overboard.

State-Sponsored Terrorist Objectives and Targets

The targets of state-sponsored terrorist organizations are similar to those of the dissident terrorist. This stems from the fact that the two types of terrorism can be similar in their goals, differing only in how the organization originated or garners support.

In many ways, state-sponsored terrorism objectives and targets vary from dissident terrorism objectives and targets by degree or severity. State-sponsored groups are willing to "go big"; the PLO supported the hijacking of international airliners as well as the cruise ship *Achille Lauro.*

International and Transnational

International terrorism is best defined as individual members from one country acting specifically against people another country, usually to influence policy or political relationships. The litany of state-on-state adversarial relationships abound: Ireland v. England, Israel v. Palestine, India v. Pakistan, South Korea v. North Korea, the United States v, Canada, so there is no shortage of people from one country ready to perpetrate violence on another country (just kidding about United States v. Canada, we wanted to see if you were awake).

In the case of international terrorism, the actor may or may not be state sponsored. We talked earlier about Palestine as an example of a state sponsors of terror, and many of its actions were directed at either Israel or the United States. In the case of the Irish Republican Army, many of their actions against England clearly occurred without any type of state sponsorship. In the case of the IRA, groups of citizens banded together for political change, some of whom resorted to violence as a tool to coerce change. What is important about these examples is that actors from one country, and one country only, acted against people or symbols in another country.

A Complicated Case Study: 2008 Mumbai Attacks

In 2008 a Pakistani terrorist organization called Lashkar-e-Taiba attacked 11 different targets in the Indian city of Mumbai. The attacks were extraordinarily violent and included random shootings of people on the street, outside a police station, and in a famous luxury hotel. The hotel attack lasted three days, becoming the ultimate symbol of what would be known as the *Mumbai Attacks,* which resulted in the death of 164 people, with only one terrorist survivor. This is where it gets weird: Lashkar-e-Taiba may have had support from the Pakistan ISI (Inter-Services Intelligence agency), which could be described as a violent shadow government behind Pakistan's official leaders. If Lashkar-e-Taiba did have support from Pakistan, it changes this act of *international terrorism* into one that could be considered *state-sponsored terrorism*, which could have redefined the Mumbai attacks as an act of war.

To make things even more complicated, and to ultimately help in defining terror groups, we also have **transnational terrorism**. When there are terrorists who are from several different nations who get together to perpetrate acts of violence against another country, you get transnational terrorism. The best example of this can be found in the 9/11 attacks by al Qaeda. In the case of 9/11, you have perpetrators from multiple counties including Egypt, Saudi Arabia, Lebanon, and the United Arab Emigrants (UAE). They came together and attacked a country other than their own—the United States—making 9/11 a transnational event. What is also significant about transnational terror groups is they are not tied to any particular country. While they operate internationally, and may be given safe haven in some terror-supporting countries, they are never identified as state sponsored.

Religious Terrorism

We all have that little voice in our head that helps us make decisions or solve problems; in the case of religious terrorism, that voice might be a little louder. **Religious terrorism** is terrorism motivated by another-worldly belief that has sanctioned or commanded violent action for the good of the faith. All terrorists are passionate about their cause, but religious terrorists believe there is divine guidance and approval for the use of violence. This divine intervention must be present, or the ability to kill and injure people would most likely be in conflict with the religion, since almost every religion frowns upon murder.

What is important to remember about religious terrorism is the difference between the terrorist actors and the mainstream practitioners of their faith. There have been extraordinary acts of violence in the name of almost every major faith, but that does not reflect the mainstream or majority of worshipers.

Some terror groups within this category are not practitioners of mainstream religions. In two famous cases, the Aum Shinrikyo Tokyo subway bombing, and the Rajneeshee salad bar poisoning, both were religious cults. Cults are small religious movements who worship a specific figure or object, and cults sometimes combine pieces of other mainstream religions into their teachings.

In the case of Aum Shinrikyo, the leader of the religious cult prophesized the world ending and attacked the Tokyo subway in areas heavily used by government officials. The motive for the attack was never exactly clear but may have been part retribution for perceived injustices and part of an effort to draw attention to the end of the world predictions.

The case of the Rajneeshee cult provides us with one of the largest bioterrorism attacks in U.S. history. Hoping to influence local elections by eliminating a large portion of the voting population, the Rajneeshee members poisoned 10 salad bars with *salmonella* in Dalles, Oregon. There were no fatalities, but the event caused 751 people to become ill, and despite the efforts of the cult, the attack did not produce the desired election outcome.

Religious terrorism can be combined with any of the above definitions to help define a group. Both Aum Shinrikyo and the Rajneshee are examples of religious domestic terror groups. An example of a religious international organization can be found in the PLO example, and al Qaeda is an example of a transnational religious terror organization.

Religious Terrorism Objectives and Targets

Modern religious terrorists know almost no bounds in selecting targets—al Qaeda killed nearly 3,000 people on 9/11. This unlimited target selection stems from the fact that unlike dissident or state-sponsored terrorists, religious terrorist groups often have unobtainable objectives or demands. Further, the motivation of the religious terrorist is not geopolitical, but stems from a religious belief or interpreted command.

This unbridled violence is the trademark of the religious terrorist, and it results in unfettered target selection and damage. Almost anything can be a target as long as its destruction can be justified through religious interpretation. High-value civilian targets, full of innocent people, are no longer off limits.

Last, any weapon is fair game for the religious terrorist. Again, if God supports the group, why would they not use a weapon of mass destruction? When that is coupled with unrealistic or unobtainable goals, the religious terrorist begins to stretch the rational choice model that drives so many other terrorist types.

Case Study: al Qaeda

The study of al Qaeda has transformed the face of terrorism—and what makes it so fascinating is the ongoing evolution of the organization. When talking about al Qaeda, it is important to distinguish between the organization formed by bin Laden and the various other al Qaeda franchises that have sprung up to include al Qaeda in Iraq (AQI), al Qaeda in the Arabian Peninsula (AQAP) and al Qaeda in the Islamic Maghreb (AQIM). The al Qaeda that came first, the organization founded by bin Laden, was a religious terror organization organized to attack the "far enemy," which was Western countries with too much influence in the Middle East. To understand the rationality of bin Laden's thinking, you need to understand the thinkers and philosophers influencing him. (We are going to do some quick and dirty history here so forgive what we don't cover.)

After World War I the British basically carved up parts of the Middle East and forgot to pay attention to indigenous belief systems and tribal territories. For a while the British tried to rule the Kingdom of Egypt as a protectorate (around 1914–1921), but that led to mass uprisings and eventually Britain recognized Egypt as sovereign, but the British didn't leave. They continued to influence Egypt from within and vastly influenced the type of leaders and politics primarily through investment (money, money, money). By the 1920s quite a few Islamic leaders were decrying the dilution and decline of the Islamic lifestyle in Egypt. In an effort to rally together, these Islamic leaders and thinkers founded the political organization the Muslim Brotherhood in Egypt as an effort to return Egypt to an Islamist country. Hasan al Banna was the founder of the Muslim Brotherhood. He believed that the influence of the British in Egypt was corrupting faithful Muslims and urged a return to the fundamental form of Islam for the Muslim family, individual, and state. Al Banna's slogan, and one that was part of the Muslim Brotherhood was "God is our goal, the Prophet is our exemplar, the Quran is our constitution, jihad is our pathway, martyrdom is what we yearn for." The Egyptian government didn't like his rabble rousing and had him assassinated.

During this same period of anti-colonial Islamic state movement, another famous Egyptian philosopher, Sayyid Qtub, was also a noteworthy person. Also a member of the Muslim Brotherhood, Qtub was unique because he traveled to the United States for two years to study at a teaching college in Colorado. (All colleges teach you, a teaching college was a place where they trained teachers.) During his time in the United States, from 1948–1950, Qtub was horrified by the sexuality and depravity he saw, writing that women in the United States were inappropriately outspoken (in 1948? Really?). On campus Qtub was exposed to parties including alcohol—a sure sign of the hedonism and corrupting influence of the West. Qtub returned to Egypt and spread his concerns in writing saying, "If all the world were America it would undoubtedly be the disaster of humanity." Rallying against Western influences, he was imprisoned in Egypt, but not killed since the assassination of al-Banna had turned him into a martyr. While in prison, Qtub eventually wrote one of the most influential books in Islamist philosophy called *Signposts* (*Ma'alim fi -l-Tariq*, also sometimes called *Milestones*). *Signposts* that declared *any form of resistance, including extreme violence*, was appropriate to stop the corrupting influences of the West on Islam. Qtub goes further and says that to protect Islam, violent measures should not *just be waged defensively for protection, but offensively* against the enemies of Islam. (It goes without saying that bin Laden was a huge believer in Qtub's writings.) Eventually, the Egyptian government executed Qtub, but the book had already left the barn, and his work continues to influence every Islamist movement and is quoted by Islamic extremists today.

As emphasized before, many mainstream religions have extremist movements that use religious teachings, and many religions also advocate their religion as a guide to the rule of law. (Any idea how many times the word "God" appears in the Declaration of Independence? What about the U.S. Constitution?) When Islamic fundamentalism is used to advocate political rule, we call the proponents *Islamists*. Because Islamists believe in a fundamentalist or ultraconservative form of Islam, many Islamic extremists self-identify themselves as Islamists. As an example, the Muslim Brotherhood has traditionally been considered the grandfather of Islamist organizations. They believed Islam should be the exclusive lifestyle choice of Muslims, that all aspects of Muslim life should be governed by Islam, and there is no room for other styles of government or rule.

Sharia Law

Sharia is the basis for Islamic law (although it is not a strict code of laws), and it covers nearly every aspect of daily life. It literally means "path to the watering place," intending to symbolize the refreshing peace that comes to those who follow it. *Sharia* primarily comes from two sources: the *Quran* (word of God) and the *Sunnah* (the example set by the Prophet Muhammad). Interpretations of *Sharia*, whether by Islamic scholars or individuals, are called *fiqh*, and it is with the human element that the implementation of *Sharia* begins to vary significantly.

© Paul Cowan, 2013. Used under license from Shuttershock, Inc.

Bin Laden and the Need for Defining Terror Groups

From 1979–1989 the Soviets were invading and fighting a war in Afghanistan (more history—stay with us, we promise it will help your understanding). This was during the Cold War era and the United States was concerned that the Soviets might win control of Afghanistan, so the United States began to supply arms to the Afghani people in order to help them repel the Soviet invaders. The politics of this are a bit complicated, but basically instead of supplying arms directly to the Afghani people, which might have made our proxy war with the Soviets too obvious, we supplied arms to Pakistan (yup, through the Pakistani ISI), then the Pakistani ISI delivered the weapons to Afghanistan on our behalf.

During these shenanigans, along comes bin Laden, who says to the Pakistani ISI that he wants to fight against the Soviets in Afghanistan, and he can put together a group of Islamic faithful, they just need weapons to do the job. (It is commonly believed bin Laden declined the training that went with the weapons.) Pakistan was excited that fighters were just showing up to help because Pakistan was in the business of moving U.S.–supplied arms to the Afghani people, but was not interested in fighting for the Afghani people. This is where you get the egg-on-face accusation that the United States supplied bin Laden with weapons, which we did, just indirectly.

(*Even* more history, stay with us) Eventually the Soviets realized they shouldn't fight a land war in Asia, and their economy back home was going broke, so they pulled out of Afghanistan. (Interesting fact: To this day no invading army has EVER taken full control of Afghanistan.) However, bin Laden had war fever and wanted to continue fighting Western invaders who threaten Islamic countries. Osama turned his attention to Saudi Arabia where the bin Laden family is from and tells the ruling Saudi royal family it is a travesty that U.S. forces have military bases on holy Saudi soil (we were invited there leading up to the Gulf War) and that he, bin Laden, wants to help the Saudis expel these Western infidels. (Think of bin Laden's offer as an effort to establish al Qaeda as *state-sponsored terrorists*). The Saudi government says, "No, thank you, we are going to let the U.S. military bases continue to be here," and bin Laden starts getting dramatic. He begins rallying people to his cause and perspective that Western countries are the "far enemy" of Islam and their presence on holy land is corrupting. The Saudi government does not take dissidents lightly and has bin Laden expelled from his homeland in 1992. Bin Laden goes to the Sudan and tries to start over, but his rabid focus on the United States as an enemy eventually gets him hustled out of Sudan as well. With nowhere else to go, bin Laden heads back to Afghanistan with his hatred of the United States solidified and plans the 9/11 attacks. Because bin Laden's al Qaeda is focused on eliminating the threat of Western influence on Islam and is targeting multiple Western countries, often using actors from multiple other countries, bin Laden's al Qaeda is a *religious transnational terror organization*.

However, when you begin to talk about al Qaeda–*affiliated groups,* the labels begin to change. If we examine the group al Qaeda in Iraq (AQI), its focus has been to expel the U.S. presence in Iraq and to topple the interim Iraqi government. AQI has been a major player in the Iraqi insurgency movement, but as its focus is strictly in Iraq, we label them differently from bin Laden's al Qaeda. If AQI exists because of the U.S. presence in Iraq, its primary label is *dissident*—it exists to repel a specific people from inside its own country. AQI's leader was Abu al-Zarqawi, who met bin Laden when they were fighting together in Afghanistan during the Soviet invasion. Both bin Laden and al-Zarqawi shared a belief of in the evil influence of the West, and before the Iraqi invasion identified the United States as the "far enemy." However, when Islamists target people or changes in their own country, their opponents are often identified as the "near enemy," so when U.S. troops entered Iraq, the far enemy became the near enemy. In addition to AQI targeting U.S. forces, they also targeted the Iraqi interim government, making AQI's focus on the near enemy. Given their actions, location, and objectives, al Qaeda in Iraq could best be defined as a *politically dissident religious terror organization.*

When we begin to examine the al Qaeda affiliate al Qaeda in the Islamic Maghreb (AQIM), we discover yet another type of organization with different goals and agenda. While all of the al Qaeda affiliates have Islamists political perspectives, AQIM is a group based in Mali that seeks to overthrow the governments of Mali and neighboring Algeria, Morocco, Nigeria, Mauritania, and Tanzania. AQIM has a regional perspective on leadership and would like to see these countries return to their Islamic roots and be governed by Islamic law. Because AQIM's focus is regional, involving multiple countries, and because the terror actors often move between these countries, it is probably fair to label them as *international religious terrorists*. The reason we wouldn't refer to AQIM actors as transnational is the presence of local fighters within many of their actions. If there are violent terror activities happening in Mali under the umbrella of AQIM, it is most likely that Mali nationals are involved in those events, even though they may have actors with them from other countries. (To confuse the issue even more, AQIM has been heavily involved in criminal enterprise throughout the regions. We will address the concept of criminal enterprise and its relationship to terrorist organizations in a subsequent chapter.)

Given the above organizations that have formally identified themselves with the version of al Qaeda formed by bin Laden, there is another type of organization we need to consider, the *ideological franchise*. We will talk more about this concept in the chapter on organizational structure and networking, but the term reflects an organic startup terror group who ideologically identifies with a larger terror organization and its message. A perfect example of an ideologically franchised terror group can be found in the London 7/7 bombing attacks. A group of four individuals banded together under the idea of Islamic extremism, and inspired by al Qaeda, perpetrated a series of bombings on public transportation systems throughout London on July 7, 2005. Despite this group's ideological support of al Qaeda, and because they were English citizens who had grown up in England and targeted their own country during their attacks, the 7/7 bombers are an example of a *domestic dissident religious* group, who acted with *ideological support* to a larger transnational terror organization. (Repeat this during a dinner conversation and you can be assured to sound well informed, and maybe even pretentious.)

Key Terms

Domestic terrorists

International terrorism

Nativism

Plausible deniability

Xenophobia

Religious terrorism

Sub-revolutionary terrorism

State-sponsored terrorism

Transnational terrorism

Discussion Questions

1. AQI exists solely because of the U.S. presence in Iraq. Does this mean that if the United States had not entered Iraq, AQI would never have been formed? Is the United States responsible for creating this terrorist organization?

2. At the beginning of AQI's formation, foreign fighters came to support its fight. Does this make a difference in the label?

3. What is another example of an ideological franchise?

References

Terrorist Threats to the United States, Testimony Before the House (House Special Oversight Panel on Terrorism May 23, 2000).

Blanchard, M. (2007). *Al Qaeda: Statements and Evolving Ideology.* Congressional Research Service, Foreign Affairs, Defense, and Trade Division. Washington, DC: Report for Congress.

Bonante, L. (1979). Some Uninted Consequences of Terrorism. *Journal of Peace Research, 16,* 197–213.

Chaliand, B. (2007). *The History of Terrorism from Antiquity to Al Qaeda.* Berkeley: University of California Press.

Laqueur, W. (1999). *The New Terrorism.* Oxford University Press.

UShistory.org. (2012, December 19). *The Sons of Liberty.* Retrieved from www.ushistory. org/declaration/related/sons.htm

Wilkinson, P. (1974). Concepts of Terror and Terrorism. In P. Wilkinson, *Political Terrorism* (pp. 13–17). New York: John Wiley.

Chapter 4

Participants in the Terrorist Event

W hen a terrorist attack occurs, news outlets and the public begin talking about who carried out the attack and the victims that were killed or injured. These are the most obvious participants in a terrorist incident (terrorist and victims), but there are more players in these events. Many of these participants are obvious and have direct roles, while others exist in the shadows and the background of media coverage. Despite the exposure granted by the media and analysts, each of these participants is critical to understanding the terrorist process and motivation—each has an important role for us to understand.

This chapter will examine the participants of a terrorist event or attack, with emphasis placed on those that exist outside the terrorist organization. It is these participants that give terrorist attacks much of their impact and power, and we must understand how they all fit together.

While we describe many participants in the terrorist event, not all will be present in every scenario. For example, some single actor or small cell terrorist organizations will have limited numbers of supporters as well as reduced influence from the terrorist organization.

The Terrorist Actor

The principal participant in a terrorist event is the terrorist himself. Much of this book examines why the terrorist chooses the path of a violent extremist, but some aspects of this choice need to be addressed in this context.

The **terrorist actor** is the person who carries out or assists with the planning of a terrorist attack. It includes all members of the terrorist organization, including those that help plan the attack, build weapons or explosives, or provide transportation or other supplies. For example, the man that plants an explosive device on a commuter train is a terrorist actor. At the same time, his associates in his terrorist organization that built the explosive device, acquired the cell phone trigger, and provided him identity documents are also terrorist actors.

A person can be classified as a terrorist actor even if the attack failed, was interdicted by authorities, or was never carried out. To qualify as a terrorist actor, the person must have the **intent** to bring violence into play. Further, this intent must be combined with the **capability** to carry out the attack. Once both of these elements are present, even if the attack never materializes, the individual is a terrorist actor.

INTENT + CAPACITY =
TERRORIST ACTOR

Courtesy of the Author

There are many terrorists in the world who never personally carry out a violent terrorist attack. Again, this definition comes down to capability and intent. A man who acquires explosive material or helps build an explosive device is building terrorist capability. At the same time, we assume that this bomb maker is aware of the intent of his work and is in agreement with the organization. This combination of capability and intent defines the man as a terrorist actor—even if he never personally uses his creation.

The same method of definition can be applied to any member of the terrorist organization that provides operational or direct support to the primary attacker. The man or woman who drives an attacker across a border or to an attack site is a terrorist actor. The person who provides travel documents or identity papers or a safe place to stay is a terrorist actor, *as long as that person understands and contributes to intent and capability*.

Without intent, without the knowledge that his or her actions will be used as part of a terrorist attack, the person cannot be a terrorist actor, but simply a supporter. Supporters will be discussed further later in this chapter.

The Terrorist Organization

The **terrorist organization** is an organizational structure that is committed to a defined cause or motivation, influences terrorist tactics and strategy, and provides a framework for planning and support. There is not a single structure for terrorist organizations; they adopt many forms, but they all have some aspects in common.

The organization's details are secret. Terrorists do not operate and exist in the open—they are hidden and obscure. While society is aware of the organization's existence (in fact, that is typically a goal of the organization), the organizational structure (with the exception of leadership or spokespersons), membership, operational rules and guidelines, and many of the organizational goals are hidden.

Without this secrecy, government law enforcement, intelligence, and military organizations would easily identify, target, and destroy the organization. Given the direct correlation between secrecy and survival, most accomplished terrorist organizations have developed elaborate methods for ensuring their secrecy while still maintaining operational capability. Without these methods, the organization soon ceases to exist.

The organization is committed to a common cause or purpose. Terrorist organizations organize around a common goal—you do not find terrorist organizations without this trait. Whether that goal or cause is politically based, ethnically or religiously motivated, or driven by territory or ideology, it is common across the organization and shared by all the members.

It is possible to have members who share differing personal goals, but they will all possess and believe in the base organizational goals. Many terrorist organizations undergo an evolutionary process regarding goals and "the cause." External and internal factors influence change, and this can result in an organization changing or evolving specific goals and causes. As an example, the inclusion of many Egyptian Islamic Jihad members into al Qaeda changed the way the original organization looked at waging jihad on a global scale. As a further example, as HAMAS gained public support and political power, the goals of the organization changed subtly from terrorist operations to politics. Similar shifts can be seen in the evolution of the Irish Republican Army (IRA) prior to the ceasefire in 1997.

Many terrorist organizations define themselves by the tactics they adopt. While these can become familiar hallmarks of an organization, many exist without these clear tactical definitions. Further, the development of tactics often depends on the cause or goal of the organization, and as such tactics change as these aspects evolve.

The organization provides support. The overall purpose of every terrorist organization is to provide support to the terrorist actors themselves. This support includes recruitment and indoctrination, training, material, money, and/or shelter.

Finally, *the organization as a whole gets the credit* for the attack. We do not say, "9/11 was a work of Atta and his band of hijackers." We attribute 9/11 to Osama Bin Laden and al Qaeda. Although individual terrorist actors carry out attacks, they are guided on their course by the organization, supported by the organization, and protected by the organization.

Supporters

Terrorists often receive support from individuals that do not qualify as being part of the terrorist's organization. These **supporters** provide both material and non-material support for the terrorist in a variety of ways, and while this support is valuable (or even critical to the terrorist), the supporter stops short of carrying out or directly enabling terrorist attacks.

There is a wide range of terrorist supporters, and the distinction between a supporter and a terrorist actor can often be very fine. For example, a man in Indiana helps acquire fertilizer that could be used to build a vehicle based improvised explosive device (VIED). He delivers this material to an acquaintance and is paid for his efforts. While he does not know explicitly that this material will be used in a terrorist attack, he has contributed directly to the capability of a terrorist organization. Some may call him a terrorist actor, but we believe that without an explicit intent to use the weapon components in an attack, this man remains a simple supporter—although a very important one (to the terrorist).

It is important for you to understand that the labels and descriptions in this chapter are academic in nature and not intended to be legal definitions. The entire point of terrorism studies is to better understand the motivations, methods, and networks of a terrorist, so that policy can be constructed to combat this global issue. Therefore, do not get mired down in the differentiations between supporter and terrorist actor from a legal or even moral point of view. The U.S. government defines providing support to terrorists as a crime and has prosecuted dozens of cases in the past decade.

Ideological Supporters

Ideology is defined as a firm set or system of beliefs and ideals. It is usually used to describe the basis of a political or social platform. As an example, most of you could easily describe the ideology that backs either the U.S. Republican or Democratic parties.

Ideological supporters have views and beliefs that align, at least partially, with the defined ideology of terrorists and terrorist organizations. This belief alignment may be based on geopolitical, religious, or other views, and it *does not have to be a complete match*. Many ideological supporters of terrorists only agree with portions of the terrorist organization's platform of beliefs; they choose and reject aspects as it suits them.

You all know an ideological supporter. Perhaps not a supporter of a terrorist organization, but the same concept applies to political parties, sports teams, and universities. That uncle you have that cheered for the sports teams of a state university despite the fact that he never attended? He's an ideological supporter of that school. What about your relative or friend who plasters her car with bumper stickers praising one political party or another? They are providing ideological support—they talk about the cause of their chosen party, they promote the party, and they defend the viewpoint of the party. All of this exists without a formal relationship between your relative and the party. That is a textbook (literally, here) case of ideological support.

Ideological supporters are easy to identify. As an example, let's look at the (fictional) Bob Smith of Florida. Smith spent 10 years in the U.S. military before being medically retired. When he returned home to his small town in rural North Florida, he got a job working as an assistant manager in a grocery store and began volunteering with the local volunteer fire department. His family all lived in the area, and the Smiths were well known throughout the county. Within a few weeks, Smith is approached by a childhood acquaintance and they strike up a renewed friendship and swap stories. Within a few days, Smith is offered a position in the local militia, which he knows is a front for the Ku Klux Klan.

While Smith doesn't disagree with the position of clan on race superiority, he doesn't feel that it is in his best interest to join the clan and actively participate in racist and dissident activity. He declines, politely, but doesn't break off his friendship with his old friend. Smith, while not willing to join the dissident (or terrorist) organization, is still an ideological supporter of the KKK. He believes and adheres to at least some of their ideological platform. He is the audience their message is aimed at, and he serves (at times, when he's had a few beers) to amplify their cause and messages to his like-minded friends.

Ideological support does not imply that the supporter agrees with the *actions* of the terrorist. Agreement with the cause or platform does not require the supporter to approve of violent activity. This reluctance to embrace violence is one of the aspects that separate the supporter from the terrorist.

Ideological supporters provide no material or financial support to the terrorist organization—so what do they do? For starters, they provide a sympathetic audience. The ideological supporter is the primary consumer of the messages being sent out by the terrorist organization. These messages could include the goals and activities of the organization, its successes, and its recruitment messages. The ideological supporter is the intended audience, and the messages are molded to appeal to this group. In turn, the messages are intended to grow the size of the ideological supporter base.

Ideological supporters also serve to amplify the messages coming from the terrorist organization. They repeat the "official" messages and use personal connections to influence others and sway their point of view. Again, you have all experienced this type of ideological support. When was the last time one of your friends of family tried to convince you of the validity of a political view of a specific party? How about the virtues of a specific sports team over another? In these examples, your friend or relative is amplifying the message originated with the organization he or she supports. In many ways, the ideological supporters of an organization function as the public relations arm of the terrorist or terrorist organization.

Ideological supporters lend weight and importance to the organization. Politicians and policymakers tend to lend more credence to the arguments and position of a terrorist organization if that organization has vocal supporters; the supporters lend legitimacy to the terrorist platform. While they don't provide material or financial support, and don't participate directly in terrorist activity, the ideological supporter is a critical part of the terrorist organization.

Financial Supporters

Terrorism requires money. It requires money to build organizations, recruit and train terrorists, travel, and buy materials, weapons, and supplies. Most terrorists and terrorist organizations cannot earn money through traditional means—jobs, etc. To fund the ongoing needs of the terrorist organization, they rely on outside support. Terrorist **financial supporters** provide money, through donations or purchase of goods and services, to terrorist organizations to fund terrorist activities.

© tandemich, 2013. Used under license from Shuttershock, Inc.

Financial supporters may not be aware they are supporting terrorist activity. After 9/11, the U. S. government promoted the fact that many terrorist organizations worldwide use the narcotics trade as a method of raising funds. The goal was to raise awareness that the purchase of illegal drugs in the United States could help fund those who wished to hurt the United States. These assertions may have been based on fact, but they were largely ineffective in curbing illicit drug use, so they were soon dropped.

Are you looking for a new vacation opportunity? Maybe you should try "jihad tourism," as long as you don't mind being arrested at some point in your journey. *Jihad tourism*, as a term, has its roots in Great Britain and is used to describe British citizens who travel to Africa or the Middle East to attend terrorist training camps.

What sets these tourists apart from being actual terrorists is, once again, a matter of intent. For jihadi tourists, the training they receive is entertainment; they never intend to put their "skills" to use. However, even if they don't carry out violent attacks, they are acting as financial and material supporters of the terrorist organization. After all, like any good tour company, the terrorists charge for the opportunity to experience the terrorist lifestyle.

For those U.S. citizens thinking of experimenting with this new vacation experience, it comes with an added authentic experience at no extra charge: arrest and prosecution for providing material support to a terrorist organization.

There are charities and other organizations that funnel money to terrorist organizations. Again, since 9/11, the United States has focused on religious schools and charities that collect money in the United States and send those funds to Islamic extremists overseas. This practice is not new, and it did not start with al Qaeda and its affiliates. Throughout the late 20th century, it was accepted that many bars, establishments, and charities in Irish neighborhoods in the United States were collecting money to support the Irish Republican Army (IRA). This practice was often disguised as fundraisers for Sein Fein, the IRA's political party in Ireland, or for a variety of schools or charitable organizations in Ireland. Anyone who participated in these types of fundraisers was considered a financial supporter of terrorism.

Just like ideological supporters, it is not necessary for a willing financial supporter to agree 100% with the terrorist's or terrorist organization's ideology or platform. However, it is typical (and logical) that a financial supporter is also an ideological supporter. People seldom give money to causes they do not agree with. We must remember, however, that some financial supporters do not know they are supporting terrorism. In these cases, the unwilling financial supporter may *not* be an ideological supporter as well.

Logistical or Material Supporters

The last level of support is logistical or material support. These individuals provide direct material support to terrorists and terrorist organizations, including physical supplies, weapons, ammunition, explosives, recruits, medicine, clothing, and other items. The U.S. government classifies anyone who sends money, either knowingly or unknowingly, to terrorist organization as a **material or logistical supporter**. While this is a valid interpretation, for this text, we are going to break the two out as separate categories. The reason we do this is that material support, while it may include financial support, indicates a higher level of support and ideological buy in. Further, it is almost impossible to be an unknowing or unwilling material supporter.

The material supporter is the top tier of terrorist supporter. These individuals fully adhere to the ideological platform and willingly know that their support will result in violent actions. There is a very fine line between being a material or logistical supporter and adopting the mantle of terrorist actor.

The United States routinely arrests and prosecutes citizens for providing material support to terrorist organizations. As mentioned in the text, the U.S. government defines a wide range of activities as material support, including those that we classify as financial or even ideological support. This distinction doesn't matter to us academically, but if you plan on studying law, expect different definitions in your future.

One example of U.S. prosecution is Randy Wilson, who was 25 at the time of his arrest in 2012. Wilson, a U.S. citizen, was accused of plotting to travel to Mauritania via Casablanca and join a violent jihad against the United States. Randy, also known as Rasheed Wilson, was arrested with Mohammad Abdul Rahman Abukhdair, also

25. Abukhadair and Wilson are both U.S. citizens living in Mobile, Alabama, and were arrested for the act of providing material support to an enemy of the United States. In this instance, the material support they intended to supply was themselves; not a small contribution. Given the media savvy of modern Islamic terrorist organizations, the recruitment of two U.S. citizens from Alabama would be a move that could be exploited in the media for years to come. Even if these two terrorists never raised a weapon against the United States, the simple act of joining the jihad against the United States would be an ongoing recruitment boon. (Federal Bureau of Investigation, 2012)

The three layers of support—ideological, financial, and material/logistical—require increasing levels of commitment to the cause. This escalation acts as a filter on the number of active supporters of each type a terrorist organization will have. Ideological supporters are the most common; there are relatively fewer financial supporters (including unwilling financial supporters), and the least amount of material or logistical supporters.

Victims

When we look at terrorist events in the light of history, we focus on two groups—the attackers and the victims. Unfortunately, we often overlook many of those who are victims of a terrorist attack, particularly one that is well documented and publicized by the media.

Every semester, we ask our students, "Where were you on September 11th?" We don't even have to include the year—everyone knows what we are talking about. At the same time, everyone (at least in 2012) could answer that question. Since the authors are older than they would like to admit, they don't like to think about the day when new university juniors or seniors don't remember that day.

The answers given range widely: from "Mrs. Edmunds' fourth-grade class" to "sitting in my office in a high rise in Chicago, wondering if we were next." The point is, everyone remembers where he or she was, just as those of a previous generation know where they were when President Kennedy was assassinated. Some have clear memories—I was driving to work after arguing with a contractor about the new kitchen counters being installed in my house, and originally dismissed the reports as "some jackass in a Cessna just managed to hit the tallest building in New York? That's unbelievable." Of course, the fact that it was unbelievable didn't deter me from believing it. When I was told by our office manager that a second plane had hit another tower, I dismissed her, thinking that she misunderstood the news reports. After all, one jackass I could understand—two was unthinkable. Only after the radio began reporting that the aircraft were airliners did I realize that we were not watching the reports of an accident—something truly monstrous had occurred.

In many ways, on that autumn morning, thousands of miles from any of the violence and terror, I was a victim. That was the entire point. We had no TV in our office, and within minutes all the news sites on the Internet were brought down due to high traffic. I drove to our local Best Buy and stood in the back of the store with dozens of others, watching NBC report on what it knew (and didn't know). We stood there and watched the towers come down on 20-foot TV screens, and more than one person around me cried. We were all victims.

No one in my town died. I did not personally know anyone who was killed that day. The largest direct issue I had was increased security and random checks when flying commercially after air traffic resumed. Despite this lack of direct effect, I was a victim. Many scholars and sociologists argue that 9/11 was such a massive event that just about everyone in the United States (and many beyond) was a victim of one description or another. Again, that was the point.

Targeted and Primary Victims

The easiest victims to indentify in a terrorist attack are those were directly targeted by the terrorist. Those that are killed are wounded in the attack are clearly identified as **primary victims**, even if they were bystanders or unintended victims of the attacker.

Nations and organizations can be primary victims as well. In the 2008 Mumbai attacks, the killed and wounded were citizens of India and tourists from a variety of nations. However, the target of the attack was the government of India, not the people who died in the attack. This may seem like a useless and academic position, until you consider the rational motivations of the terrorist. In order to draw attention to his actions, the terrorist chooses a target that is symbolic and then perpetrates an attack of extraordinary violence against that target. This attack results in primary victims—those killed and wounded in the terrorist event.

In the traditional academic view, as espoused by Brian Jenkins in 1975, "Terrorists want a lot of people watching and a lot of people listening and not a lot of people dead." In other words, primary victims are necessary to attract the public's attention, but too many and the terrorist runs the risk of turning his audience against him. This view took a serious blow on 9/11 and in the years that followed, when no scenario was considered unthinkable. Nuclear terrorism, biological and chemical weapons, coordinated suicide bombing attacks all seemed equally possible in small-town America.

The government counterterrorism view in the wake of 9/11 portrayed a terrorist willing to kill hundreds, thousands, or even hundreds of thousands—just because he could.

Primary victims include spouses, children, family, and friends of those killed or wounded in the attack. These indirect victims suffer greatly in the aftermath of an attack (particularly if their family member or friend was killed) and often require extensive support to return to a normal life.

Secondary Victims

Secondary victims primarily include responders and other operational personnel who deal with the aftermath of a violent attack. While there is a public perception that firefighters, emergency medical technicians, and law enforcement personnel are equipped to deal with the trauma and violence of a terrorist attack, the reality is that these events can be overwhelming.

In some particularly traumatic events, members of the media may fall into the category of secondary victims. As they deal with responders, work in close proximity of the attack site, and discuss the event with primary and other secondary victims, media members encounter massive amounts of stress. This stress can easily approach the levels that first responders and on scene personnel deal with and can be just as destructive.

After the Murrah Federal Building bombing in Oklahoma City in 1995, almost 12,000 first responders and volunteers participated in the initial search and rescue and the subsequent search and recovery efforts. Within hours of the blast that killed 167, including 19 children, local officials and the American Red Cross had established a Compassion Center for victim and family assistance. Staffed by local crisis professionals, military chaplains, religious leaders, and crisis counseling volunteers from around the United States, the Compassion Center was originally established to serve the needs of primary victims of the bombing.

It was quickly recognized that many of the responders were in need of crisis counseling services, and the Compassion Center expanded its offerings to include services for those working in and around the site. Open for over two weeks, the Compassion Center served thousands of primary and secondary victims and became a hub for information and comfort. (Office for Victims of Crime, 2000)

It is important to recognize and meet the post-crisis needs of these secondary victims. It has become common practice to monitor the post-crisis well-being of response personnel and other operational entities. This type of monitoring, followed by the provision of mental health assistance, can limit the effect of being a secondary victim.

Global Victims

Catastrophic events such as the 9/11 attacks create indirect victims around the world. These **global victims** may not be located anywhere near the site of the violence, but witness and experience it via media coverage. This second-hand exposure can be traumatic to the global victim and contribute to feelings of lost security and anxiety.

Two developments in the past 10 or 12 years exacerbate this situation. First, as terrorism evolves and embraces greater levels of violence (see Chapter 5), the shock and horror experienced by the global victims increases. 9/11 was a traumatic event for many people across the nation and world, despite the fact that very few were in close proximity to the actual incident sites. We see similar levels of long-distance trauma in relation to other events such as the 7/7 bombings in London and even the Oklahoma City bombing in 1995. Each of these events was beyond the scope of "normal" terrorist activities, and had a wide impact on the mental health of citizens.

Social media serves as an amplifier to terrorist attacks and can widen the area where global victims can be found. Even when an event is covered heavily by the traditional media, social networks can add a personal connection to an already traumatic story. If a person is not directly affected (she is not a primary or secondary victim), it is possible that a friend of a friend (of a friend) may be. At this point, stories and photos of the victims begin to spread on social media outlets, creating a sense of connection and loss. It is easy to sympathize with your best friend Joan's neighbor who lost a cousin in the attack. This sense of connection in social media can greatly enlarge the pool of global victims.

Economic Victims

Our final distinct category of victims involves financial loss. Terrorist attacks, particularly major attacks in urban centers, can create massive direct financial loss from physical damage, infrastructure damage and disruption, and transportation issues. All of these losses are passed on to someone, somewhere. Even if governments pay for most of the direct recovery, those costs are borne by taxpayers and others.

When the World Trade Center was attacked on 9/11, over 15,000 businesses in Manhattan were either destroyed completely or had their operations disrupted. The loss of these businesses (ranging from small shops to multimillion-dollar companies) resulted in direct job losses and a reduction in the economy of New York City, New York State, and the United States. These economic losses created a wide web of **economic victims** of the attack.

While 9/11 is a dramatic and wide-scale example of economic victims, any terrorist attack will have direct and indirect economic victims. Stock markets fall in the aftermath of terrorist attacks. Businesses are destroyed or damaged and job are lost. People without employment spend less on food, clothing, and entertainment—there is a trickle-down effect.

In the United States, the federal government provides assistance to those impacted by disasters and terrorist attacks. This aid comes primarily through the Small Business Administration (SBA), which makes low-interest loans available to businesses and homeowners to cover cash flow issues and rebuilding costs. While the SBA loan programs are critical to recovery and viewed favorably by most analysts, there is a cost passed on to taxpayers to administer the program as well as costs associated with loans not repaid by borrowers. Again, taxpayers and citizens become indirect economic victims.

Interpreters

In the aftermath of a terrorist attack, the media is filled with individuals explaining what happened, why it happened, how it happened, and what happens next. These people are attempting to add a layer of meaning and context to the terrorist event, and we call them **interpreters**.

Interpreters play a key role in the terrorist event. They attempt to take the chaos and aftermath of a violent terrorist attack and provide meaning for their audience. Most interestingly, interpreters craft their message to fit the needs of their audience, and they do this both consciously and unconsciously. Two separate interpreters will interpret the same terrorist event, with the same set of published facts, differently. For example, a terrorist bombing of a nightclub in Europe will be looked at and talked about very differently by a German and American newspaper. Each of these interpreters formats and highlights portions of the actual events to suit the audience they are serving.

This **bias** exists everywhere and should be recognized and understood by citizens and scholars.

Authors and Academics

Academics and authors have been trying to explain terrorism and terrorist events for decades, and that trend accelerated in the past decade. You're reading this book right now, aren't you? The hallmark of the academic interpretation of terrorism is this: Terrorists are rational actors carrying out rational acts. Their actions may be horrific, but they are not the actions of "crazy" people bent on destruction for the sake of destruction.

This view was shaken after 9/11. Government analysts and policymakers countered that modern terrorists (particularly those motivated by religion) attacked Western nations out of hatred and rage, not rational thought. This debate continues today and is discussed in Chapter 7.

Academics write papers and textbooks. They lecture classes, and they attempt to educate using the long form. You won't find an academic studying terrorism with only a little to say on the subject. Their (our) interpretations tend to look at the causes of terrorism, why terrorism is or is not effective, and the impacts terrorism has on society.

Armchair Generals

You've all seen these analysts on television. Pressed into service (and often compensated for their time), these experts describe terrorist events and detail how the event unfolded and what the direct impacts were. This group is made up of active or prior service military, law enforcement, or intelligence professionals, and many have a large body of valuable insight to bring to the analysis and discussion.

These professionals have real-world experience that lends weight to their interpretations and arguments, and the public respects their opinions. This acceptance gives them a head start in credibility, even if they are working on limited facts or incorrect assumptions.

Policymakers and Politicians

Government officials inevitably wind up acting as interpreters for terrorist events, for a wide variety of reasons. Policymakers and professional bureaucrats, including law enforcement, intelligence, and public safety officials, are considered to be official sources of information regarding terrorism and terrorist events. As such, there is often a large degree of trust between these officials and the general public. Politicians, on the other hand, often use terrorism and terrorist events to further their political goals.

After 9/11, American politicians often used the threat of continuing international terrorism as a campaign talking point and platform component. The American public wanted to recapture some sense of the security they felt on September 10, 2001, and politicians at every level capitalized on this need to convince voters that their platform and plans were the best way to achieve this.

Policymaker interpretations of terrorism and terrorist events underwent an evolution after 9/11 in the United States. Prior to that event, analysts and policymakers used a **threat-based approach** to terrorism. The goals, methods, and projected capabilities of the terrorist organization were used to predict future attacks. This threat-based method creates limited scenarios that are within the abilities of the terrorist organizations. The drawback and failure of threat-based analysis is that it was not comprehensive or forward thinking. The 9/11 attacks, using hijacked airliners as weapons, was outside the typical terrorist pattern of action; it was completely unforeseen.

From threat-based analysis developed **vulnerability-based** terrorism studies. In this type of analysis, no terrorist attack scenario was too far-fetched for study. From biological weapons to suitcase-sized nuclear devices, every scenario was considered not only possible, but probable. Planners and analysts stopped working forward from the terrorist organization to what actions it might take and began working backwards from the defined vulnerability and/or target, assuming that an organization existed that would eventually exploit that vulnerability.

This change in counterterrorism thinking changed the way policymakers (and non-campaigning politicians) interpreted terrorist events or organizations. Almost universally, the threats faced by a society were increased and magnified, and each event became justification for further spending in defending our myriad vulnerabilities.

Facilitators

Facilitators serve as communications channels and hubs for delivering information about terrorist organizations and events. These individuals or organizations may employ or add their own interpreters, but often they simply repeat the information provided to them form official and unofficial sources.

These news outlets are critical to the terrorist. Remember, a terrorist organization carries out its violent agenda to deliver a message to society or the world. Without the facilitators, the terrorist cannot move his or her message and is neutralized.

CNN, Fox News, al Jazeera, NBC News, the BBC, and social media sites are all examples of terrorism facilitators. They would not care to be labeled as such, but the sad reality is that news coverage makes terrorism possible. The news media reports on terrorist organizations because that information is in demand and therefore sells advertising. It is for this reason that any time an Islamic terrorist organization attacks anything worldwide, it is always "affiliated with al Qaeda." Even if that connection in tenuous (or nonexistent), it will still get added to the headline because it grabs more viewers and therefore sells more advertising. This may sound cynical, but it is accurate. We will discuss the media's role in terrorism in detail in a later chapter.

Social Media as a Facilitator

Social media, particularly Facebook and Twitter, are an instantaneous source of news to the modern world. When the Mumbai attacks began in 2008, information about the event initially spread via Twitter. The information available included cell phone pictures of the events as well as quick reports of fires, explosions, and violence. These near real-time reports outpaced traditional media in reporting the events but were completely unverifiable. Further, these messages were repeated by Twitter users around the world, then spread to other social media platforms (such as Facebook), then to traditional media. As these messages spread, these stories were thought to have been endorsed by the person repeating the information. If the receiver of these messages trusted the sender (who was repeating information), then the receiver may trust the message as being accurate and verified—this unintentional **endorsement** of repeated messages created an illusion of authenticity.

This illustrates both the power and flaws of social media as a terrorism facilitator. Messages can spread quickly, but the unverified or untrue information can be perceived (through unintentionally endorsement) as factual. This type of relayed, peer-to-peer communication can create a web of inaccurate data very quickly. Despite these weaknesses, the power of social media as a communication medium cannot be ignored.

Social People

If you gather five people together and ask about a terrorist event, everyone will have a unique opinion on the event, the perpetrator, and the motivations. Many of these opinions will be wrong, but that will not prevent them from being spread in a social setting.

Classic "water cooler" conversation in an office environment can function like a primitive Twitter or social network website. Information is received (via traditional media, social media, friends, or family), then repeated to others in a social setting. From there that information will be spread to others, and in the process it will undergo transformation. Most face-to-face communication includes some aspect of interpretation as well as simple facilitation. Opinions and insight will blend into the factual information, some of it accurate and useful, some of it not.

There are many participants in the terrorist event, ranging from the terrorist actor to the media reporting on the incident. Each of these participants plays a critical role in how the event is viewed and understood. The terrorist organization and the victims are often the most visible, but they also have a very short timeline in the event. The longest exposure comes from the interpreters and facilitators, who convey meaning and descriptions of the incident to the general public. Each of these is important to the terrorist, as they all help convey the overall terrorist message.

Not all participants are present in all terrorist events. Many modern terrorist attacks are carried out by so called **lone wolf** terrorists. These **single actor** terrorist events can occur without any organization as a direct participant, although you will often find an organization on the periphery, acting as an ideological or material supported to the terrorist.

Key Terms

Bias	Lone wolf
Capability	Material or logistical supporter
Economic victim	Primary victim
Endorsement	Secondary victim
Facilitators	Single actor
Financial supporter	Supporters
Global victim	Terrorist actor
Ideological supporter	Terrorist organization
Ideology	Threat-based analysis
Intent	Vulnerability-based analysis
Interpreters	

Discussion Questions

1. Why does the media, including social media platforms such as Facebook, serve as mediators for terrorist activity?

2. Can an ideological supporter ever change his or her stance on the issues? Can he or she advance past the supporting role to a more active position?

3. Which of the supporters are most important to the terrorist organization? Why?

4. Could terrorism exist as we know it today without the media?

References

Federal Bureau of Investigation. (2012, December 11). *Alabama Men Arrested on Terrorism Charges*. Retrieved January 22, 2013, from Federal Bureau of Investigation: www.fbi.gov/mobile/press-releases/2012/alabama-men-arrested-on-terrorism-charges

Office for Victims of Crime. (2000). *Responding to Terrorism Victims, Oklahoma City and Beyond*. U.S. Department of Justice. Washington, DC: U.S. Department of Justice.

Chapter 5

Weapons and Tactics

This chapter discusses some of the "tools of the trade" of terrorism. We don't like to get into great detail about this in the classroom because we avoid, as much as possible, the feeling of providing any "hands-on" instruction in terrorism. However, these tools are often misunderstood, overestimated, and underestimated, so we are going to take some space to discuss them so you can understand the reality of what a terrorist can and cannot do. There is a tendency in terrorism studies to overestimate the capabilities of terrorists, and this trend has been sharply present since 9/11. We must be cautious in our analysis and study—terrorist elements can be a threat to our society but we must take care not to inflate these threats.

Weapons

Conventional Weapons

A typical terrorist attack is carried out using an explosive, a firearm, or other conventional weapon. It is easy to imagine a terrorist with a massive explosive device, a chemical weapon, or even a radiological device, but the reality is typically much simpler. For the purposes of this study, we will divide terrorist weapons into two categories—**conventional weapons** (such as firearms, knives, grenades, most explosives, etc.) and weapons of mass destruction (WMDs). Most terrorists would like to have access to the latter category, but that scope of weapon is not easy to acquire, maintain, or employ. Despite this, conventional weapons can be put to terrifying use—even a simple machete can be used as a terrorist weapon. We cannot forget that the 9/11 hijackers used box cutters—knives—to carry out an attack that killed nearly 3,000 Americans. While we must think and plan for a WMD attack, we cannot ignore the simple weapons.

Melee Weapons

A melee weapon requires the user to be in close proximity or contact with the victim; knives, machetes, clubs, and other melee weapons are commonly used in terrorist attacks. Although they lack the visceral impact of an explosion, they can be hidden easily and used to great effect in crowded areas. Further, they are simple to obtain, inexpensive, and require little or no training to use.

Firearms

Firearms of all types are common terrorist weapons. This popularity can be attributed to two factors: availability and effectiveness. A terrorist operating in just about any region of the world will be able to obtain one or more firearms. When this ease of acquisition is combined with the fact that any firearm makes a single individual terrorist capable of killing or wounding dozens of people in a short amount of time, it is no wonder that firearms and explosives are the most common terrorist weapons.

Handguns, or sidearms, are designed to be used with a single hand, are easy to carry or conceal, and are typically useful in short-range encounters, such as inside a building or aircraft. They can be holstered on the belt, stashed in a pocket or backpack, or stored in a handbag or vehicle glove box. Handguns come in a variety of types, including revolvers (which typically hold six rounds of ammunition in an internal cylinder) and pistols (which feed rounds of ammunition from a magazine, typically located in the grip of the weapon). Revolvers are *semiautomatic*; each pull of the trigger fires one round of ammunition. The vast majority of pistols are semiautomatic, although a very few, such as the Glock Model 18, are fully *automatic*; the weapon will continue to fire as long as the trigger is depressed. In the United States, access to automatic weapons is restricted to persons licensed by the federal government to possess them. Other developed countries have similar or tougher firearms laws.

Rifles are fired from the shoulder and typically use higher-powered ammunition than handguns. The added length, power, and stability make rifles more effective at longer ranges, which is useful in outdoor environments. Rifles may be semiautomatic, automatic, single-shot (requiring a single round of ammunition to be loaded into the weapon for each shot), bolt-action (requiring the user to manually chamber a round from a magazine between shots), or lever-action (similar to bolt action, except the user manipulates a lever at the bottom of the rifle to chamber or load a new round).

© zimand, 2013. Used under license from Shuttershock, Inc.

"The AK-47"

One of the most common rifles used by terrorist organizations is the AK-47 and its many variants. The AK-47 was designed in the Soviet Union in 1946 as the primary rifle of the Soviet Army. It fires a 7.62x39mm round from a 30-round magazine and is capable of semi-automatic or automatic operation; firearms that have this capability are called *select-fire weapons*. The AK-47 is popular with militaries and terrorists around the world for three reasons. First, it is inexpensive. The Soviet designer of the AK-47, Mikhail Kalashnikov, never thought to patent the rifle's design, making it the most reproduced and counterfeited weapon in the world. Second, it is easy to use and maintain; it is said that the AK-47 is the most forgiving firearm in the world. You can mistreat it, drop it, get it dirty, forget to oil it, and it will still fire when the trigger is pulled. Last, the AK-47 fires a cheap, plentiful, and powerful cartridge.

In the United States, it may appear that you can go to your local gun show or gun shop and purchase an AK-47. In fact, you cannot. You can purchase a version of the AK-47 that has one significant difference—it has no automatic fire capability; it is semiautomatic only. These rifles may appear the same as the venerable AK, but they lack many of the features and capabilities.

Rifles have a variety of purposes and configurations. An army infantryman may carry a select-fire rifle into battle, and a civilian hunter may carry a very similar semiautomatic rifle to hunt deer or small game. A high-powered bolt-action rifle may be used to hunt large game, and a very similar weapon could be employed by a sniper to engage targets at ranges up to a mile. This versatility makes rifles effective terrorist weapons.

Submachine guns are similar to rifles, except they are chambered to fire pistol ammunition such as the 9x19mm Parabellum or the .45 ACP (Automatic Colt Pistol). These weapons are typically select-fire and are popular with police forces for their relatively low power (compared to rifles) and ease of use. Submachine guns are typically shorter and lighter than a rifle, which makes them easier to conceal. This makes them popular with terrorists as well. More modern submachine guns are chambered for advanced ammunition designed to penetrate body armor. These weapons (and their ammunition) are restricted and difficult to obtain.

Machine guns are large, fully automatic weapons designed for sustained rates of fire. These weapons are heavy and difficult to conceal but fire powerful ammunition, ranging from rifle calibers such as 5.56mm or 7.62mm up to the .50 caliber round, which is capable of penetrating and destroying a vehicle engine. Machine guns are not typically found in civilian hands, nor are they commonly used by police forces. Machine guns are a potent weapon on the battlefield, and this capability makes them popular with terrorist organizations as well.

Shotguns were originally sporting weapons, designed for hunting birds and other game. They have become military weapons in the past hundred years and come in a variety of types. The majority of shotguns are semiautomatic, with a capacity of four to eight rounds of ammunition. Some recent military shotguns are magazine fed and are capable of automatic fire, although these are rare and can be difficult to obtain.

This description of different types of firearms is not meant to be exhaustive, but is intended to illustrate the large variety of firearms available to terrorist elements. Remember, when discussing the availability of these weapons to terrorists, we are not talking about stepping out to a sporting goods store and purchasing a firearm off the rack. The perceived "gun problem" in the United States has nothing to do with terrorism. A terrorist organization, many of whom have state support, can obtain weapons on the international arms markets, without concern for national laws or restrictions.

Explosives

Explosives account for the majority of terrorist attacks worldwide. Despite the increased concern in the United States and other nations about chemical, biological, or radiological weapons, history shows terrorists overwhelmingly prefer conventional explosives and firearms for their attacks. Explosives can take many forms, from crude homemade devices to advanced commercial or military explosives. This section will attempt to clarify some of the types and their origin.

© GLYPHstock, 2013. Used under license from Shuttershock, Inc.

"U.S. military hand grenades"

One of the simplest forms of explosive weapon is the grenade. **Hand grenades** are designed to be easily portable and have an effective range of about 5 meters from the blast. Grenades are made all over the world, but share some similar characteristics. The user must first remove or disable a safety device (often a "pin"), then manually start the fuse or the fuse is initiated automatically when the grenade is released from the hand. Fuse times vary, but can range from three to six seconds before the grenade explodes. The outer casing of the grenade is designed to become **shrapnel**, fast-moving metal fragments intended to maim or kill. Grenades are popular terrorist weapons because they are easy to carry and conceal, they are simple to use, and the public easily recognizes them. In that manner, grenades become an effective **threat weapon**—intended to coerce behavior from the public.

Rocket-propelled grenades (RPGs) are shoulder-fired **rockets** designed to destroy or disable light vehicles, such as trucks, personnel carriers, or automobiles. Terrorists often employ RPGs to ambush or attack people in civilian vehicles, or to destroy barricades or other obstacles to gain entry to an area.

© Aydin Bacak, 2013. Used under license from Shuttershock, Inc.

"The common rocket-propelled grenade launcher, without a grenade loaded"

Ammonium Nitrate and Fuel Oil

ANFO is a commonly used industrial explosive for mining and construction applications. It is a free-flowing granular mixture of ammonium nitrate (AN) and fuel oil (FO) that is low cost and ease-of-use makes it the most popular industrial explosive in North America—it accounts for approximately 80% of explosives used annually.

ANFO is a particularly simple explosive to reproduce with generic, nonexplosive materials. Widely available ammonium nitrate blend fertilizer and diesel fuel, for instance, have been a popular formula for improvised explosive devices (IEDs), although devices made with agricultural-grade AN are of lower yield than those made with explosive-grade AN. Improvised ANFO was the explosive utilized in the 1993 World Trade Center bombing. A variant of ANFO was also used in the 1995 Oklahoma City bombing.

Commercial explosives are used in a variety of manufacturing, mining, and excavation purposes and include materials such as dynamite, TNT, and the plastic explosive **Semtex**. Commercial explosives are sometimes easier to obtain than military-grade explosives, and will work just as well for a terrorist weapon.

Semtex

Semtex is a plastic-explosive with mining, construction, and military applications. Semtex contains RDX (Research Department Explosive) and PETN (Pentaerythritol tetranitrate), two of the highest-yield explosives currently in use. RDX and PETN are combined with plasticizers to form a malleable, semisolid, waterproof explosive compound.

Semtex is suspected in many terrorist events due to the fact that hundreds of pounds of it were exported directly from the manufacturer in Europe to Libya in the late 1970s. Further, Semtex does not require sophisticated blasting cap or detonator technologies, and was, until recently, difficult to detect.

Military explosives are designed explicitly for use by military organizations, typically in large caliber shells (such as artillery rounds) or aircraft munitions (bombs). Compound military explosives such as RDX are potent weapons, but difficult to obtain. A famous military explosive is the compound plastic explosive Composition 4, or C-4. Semtex and C-4 are similar and relatively stable making them difficult to detonate accidentally. This stability, when combined with their plastic (malleable) shape, makes them an ideal explosive weapon for a terrorist attack. Hidden in luggage or in a vest worn under clothing, plastic explosives can be difficult to detect and devastatingly effective.

"Molotov cocktail, lit and ready to throw"

The "**Molotov cocktail**" is a famous name for a **gasoline or alcohol bomb**. These incendiary devices are constructed of a glass container filled with a highly flammable liquid such as gasoline or high-proof alcohol. A rag or wick is used to stopper the bottle and then lit on fire. The flaming device is hurled at the target, shattering the glass container. The flame ignites the reserve of accelerant liquid, which in turn sets fire to the area. The weapon is simple to construct from a variety of readily available materials, which makes it another popular terrorist weapon. To be clear, the Molotov cocktail is not an explosive, but an incendiary device—designed to quickly cover a target area in flame; there is no detonation or explosion.

Explosive weapons require a **trigger device** to start the explosive reaction. While some explosives or compounds, are unstable and easy to detonate (such as nitroglycerin), other explosive compounds require considerable force, such as a smaller explosion, to detonate. Despite these differences, each explosive requires a trigger, and these are often more complicated to create than Hollywood movies would make us believe.

A **fuse** is the simplest trigger device, and most of you are familiar with them from bottle rockets and firecrackers you played with on the Fourth of July. A modern fuse is a length of readily combustible material that carries a flame from the point of ignition to the explosive. The length of a fuse can also serve as a timer, and provides the bomber with adequate time (in theory) to escape the blast. Fuses are often waterproof and windproof, but the flame they transfer is not sufficient to detonate complicated explosives such as C4 or Semtex.

Timers may be constructed of clocks, watches or specialized components, and they all serve the same purpose—provide the attacker the time needed to get away from the device before it detonates. This time may be a few seconds or minutes, providing a terrorist the time to escape the blast, or may be hours or days, to allow the armed device to be in an advantageous position. For example, if the explosive is placed on an aircraft, a timer may allow the plane to take off and reach altitude before the weapon explodes.

The Lockerbie Bombing: Pan Am Flight 103

On December 12, 1988, Pan Am Flight 103 lifted off from the London Heathrow Airport headed to New York. An hour into the flight, a device concealed in a piece of checked luggage exploded near the front of the 747-400 aircraft. The explosion caused the nose section of the aircraft to separate from the rest of the fuselage, and both sections fell to earth.

The remains of the aircraft crashed into Lockerbie, Scotland, where the wreckage and remaining jet fuel destroying several houses and killed 11 people on the ground. All 259 people on board were killed.

The explosive was determined to be concealed inside a stereo cassette recorder and was fashioned of Semtex, a commercial plastic explosive (ee breakout box). The device had an electronic timer that allowed the plane to reach cruising altitude before the explosion was triggered. With Flight 103 flying at approximately 31,000 feet, even a relatively small device had catastrophic consequences.

A three-year investigation by Scottish and American authorities revealed that Libyan intelligence operatives had designed and carried out the attack on the airliner. A large quantity of Semtex was exported to Libya in the late 1970s, and the timer was similar in type to one previously confiscated from a Libyan intelligence operative. Two Libyan men were indicted in 1991 and turned over by the Libyan government in 1999. While Libyan leader Muammar Qaddafi admitted his government's involvement in the attack, he never took personal responsibility. With his death in 2011, the extent of his direct involvement may not ever be known.

Trigger devices may be more complex than a simple timer. Authorities have recovered triggers that respond to contact pressure and detonate when they are touched or disturbed, as well as triggers that activate when moved. Remote or radio triggers allow an attacker to detonate the device on command from a safe distance. These radio triggers can be made specifically for use as detonators, but can also be improvised from portable radios and cellular phones.

Weapons of Mass Destruction (WMDs)

If you discuss terrorism and the United States, you cannot avoid the topic of **weapons of mass destruction** or **WMD**s. Policymakers, politicians, and the media all appear to be incapable to talking about terrorism without using the term. While the majority of terrorist attacks use conventional, even mundane, weapons, there is concern about a terrorist organization acquiring a functional WMD, specifically a chemical, biological, or nuclear weapon. The use, or even a threat of use, would strike fear into the hearts of a targeted population. The problem from a policy standpoint is, as we are about to discuss, that the category of WMD has been diluted and stretched to the point that it is virtually meaningless.

What is a WMD, anyway?

In March 2013, the United States charged Eric Harroun of Phoenix, Arizona, with conspiring to use a destructive device outside of the United States. This charge stems from the fact that Harroun was fighting with rebels in Syria against the Al-Assad regime and was part of a team firing rocket-propelled grenades. The specifics of Harroun's case are murky at best, but it illustrates some interesting definitions in federal law (Shane, 2013).

Harroun was charged under Title 18 United States Code, Chapter 113B, Section 2332a, which states: "Any national of the United States who, without lawful authority, uses, or threatens, attempts, or conspires to use, a weapon of mass destruction outside of the United States shall be imprisoned for any term of years or for life, and if death results, shall be punished by death, or by imprisonment for any term of years or for life." The section goes on to define a weapon of mass destruction as "(A) any destructive device as defined in section 921 of this title; (B) any weapon that is designed or intended to cause death or serious bodily injury through the release, dissemination, or impact of toxic or poisonous chemicals, or their precursors; (C) any weapon involving a biological agent, toxin, or vector (as those terms are defined in section 178 of this title); or (D) any weapon that is designed to release radiation or radioactivity at a level dangerous to human life" (United States Code, 2012).

The definition includes some familiar components—chemical, biological, and radiological weapons, but also refers to section 921 of the same title for an expansion on the definition of "destructive devices." It turns out that section 921 includes a wide variety of devices that are considered (by reference) as weapons of mass destruction. These include "any explosive, incendiary, or poison gas," "grenade," "rocket having a propellant charge of more than four ounces," and any "device similar to any of the devices described" (United States Code, 2012). In effect, any explosive of any size, any hand grenade, an RPG, and a Molotov cocktail are all classified as weapons of mass destruction.

The disposition of Harroun's case won't be final until long after this text goes to press, but that is not what interests us. If the man is guilty of the alleged crimes, he should be punished. However, to equate the use of an RPG to the use of a nuclear weapon is asinine. In the eyes of the public, we are inflating the threat from mundane weapons while at the same time minimizing the threat from legitimate WMDs.

Why are we seeing this inflation of the threats? Why is a shoulder-fired RPG classified the same as a nuclear weapon? The trend may be reflective of our ever-present fear (as a society) of terrorism. We still see 9/11 in our collective consciousness, and we do not want to face that kind of terrorism at home ever again. What does that say about the fear we have of a nuclear (or biological or chemical) attack that we would haphazardly classify it as the same as a person carrying an RPG or hand grenade? Are we trying to amplify the modest threat, or are we trying to reduce the appearance of a threat from a nuclear weapon?

In this text, the only "weapons of mass destruction" are nuclear, chemical, biological, and radiological devices. Even these "big four" are not equal in terms of potential for destruction, casualties, and financial impacts. Chemical weapons are subject to wind and weather and require densely packed victims for maximum effectiveness. Biological weapons are difficult to develop and control, and the infection paths and incubation times make it difficult to cause widespread mortality. Radiological weapons are terrifying, but their casualty rates may be low even compared to a chemical event. Only a nuclear weapon fully reaches the "weapon of mass destruction" plateau, with massive death, destruction and disruption from even a small device. Despite these wide differences in potential impact these four weapons have one single commonality: They produce incredible fear, anxiety, and uncertainty when there is a threat of their use by terrorists. This is the reason that we will group them together here, as well as the reason that we reject so many other weapons that scholars and practitioners have labeled "WMD."

Weapons of mass destruction are often referred to as **CBRN** weapons. CBRN (pronounced *see-burn*) is an acronym that represents Chemical, Biological, Radiological, and Nuclear weapons. Some analysts and organizations use **CBRNE** (pronounced *see-burn-ee*), which adds Explosive to the acronym. In that case, it refers only to a high-yield explosive, something like the Oklahoma City device, and not small explosive devices like grenades or rockets. A very few analysts have begun adding a "T" for Technology to the acronym, to create **CBRNET** (*see-bur-net*). This reflects the growing concern over cyberterrorism and cyber attacks, although we do not feel the technological threat has crossed into the same domain as a nuclear, chemical, or radiological device. Given our stance on the inflation of the WMD term, we will stick with the traditional CBRN acronym, although we will discuss cyber threats briefly.

Chemical Weapons

Chemical weapons are defined as "any toxic chemical or its precursor that can cause death, injury, temporary incapacitation or sensory irritation through its chemical action" (Organization for the Prohibition of Chemical Weapons, 2013). This definition is straightforward and includes the **precursor materials—** compounds that when mixed create the chemical weapon or reaction. Many governments and world organizations also recognize the delivery munitions, even without a chemical present, as a chemical weapon or potential WMD. Examples of a chemical weapon delivery munitions include chemical artillery shells, systems for creating an aerosol, and pressurized spray tanks. These types of munitions have no other use than the delivery of chemical agents.

When we look at the CBRN weapons, chemical agents have the longest history of use in warfare. There are reports of cyanide usage in the Franco-Prussian War (1870–1871), and World War I saw widespread usage of a new variety of terrible chemical weapons. Chlorine, phosgene, and mustard gases were nightmare weapons of the Great War, and the successes of these weapons on the battlefield led to development of more advanced (and deadly) materials. German research into organophosphates led to the development of "nerve gases," which were tested in concentration camps, but not used on troops during WWII.

In today's environment, chemical weapons are relatively easy and inexpensive to acquire or create. These costs are in comparison to other weapons of mass destruction, making chemical agents an attractive terrorist weapon.

Chemical agents can exist and be used in solid, liquid, or gas form (for those of you with a working knowledge of the states of matter, these should look familiar), and they are classified according to their effect on the human body. We use five classifications of chemical weapons: neurotoxins, chemical asphyxiates, respiratory irritants, skin irritants, and anti-personnel agents.

Neurotoxins

Neurotoxins are nerve agents, designed to attack and disable the nervous system of the victim. These agents can enter the body through a variety of routes including inhalation, ingestion, or through skin absorption. Neurotoxins attack and shut down neurons, which exist throughout the brain and nervous system and are critical for even basic bodily functions such as respiration and swallowing. Exposure symptoms include dizziness, loss of motor control, nausea and vomiting, loss of vision, paralysis, and seizures. They can affect higher brain functions and in many cases, exposure is ultimately fatal.

Examples of neurotoxins include VX, Sarin (also known by the military designation GB), and Tabun (designated GA).

Sarin was developed in Germany in the 1930s and is an odorless and colorless liquid at room temperature. It can evaporate into an odorless gas or be delivered in an **aerosol** form (liquid droplets suspended in a mist—think of a can of hairspray). Victims can be exposed to Sarin in the air by inhaling it, skin exposure, or through the membranes in the eye.

Tabun is very similar to Sarin, and was developed around the same time in Germany. It has a slightly fruity odor, but is a tasteless, colorless liquid that can be aerosolized or heated into a vapor.

VX is considered to be the most lethal of the nerve agents. Developed in Britain in the 1950s, it is an amber-colored liquid with an oily consistency. It is slow to evaporate and is typically delivered as an aerosol form. Like Tabun and

Sarin, exposure is through inhalation, skin contact, or through the eyes, although much less VX is required for a dangerous dose. Even a drop of VX directly on the skin is enough to be fatal.

> ### Tokyo Subway Sarin Attack
>
> We have seen neurotoxins used by a terrorist organization. In 1995, the Japanese cult Aum Shrinko released Sarin into the Tokyo subway system. Five packages, consisting of plastic bags filled with liquid Sarin then wrapped in newspapers were carried onto subway trains during rush hour. The packages were dropped on the ground and punctured with umbrellas, allowing the Sarin to flow on the floor of the train or station. The puncturing of the packages was done as a train reached a station, allowing the attacker to exit the enclosed space quickly. Since the Sarin was in liquid form, it took a few minutes to begin to evaporate into a vapor, but once this happened people began to fall ill. In the final count, eight people died and over 5,000 required attention at area hospitals.
>
> The Tokyo Sarin attack clearly illustrates the allure of chemical weapons to a terrorist organization. The agent was delivered in liquid form and allowed to evaporate slowly into a vapor. This is not, by any means, the best way to deliver the agent, and had Aum Shrinko delivered the Sarin in an aerosolized form, the death toll could have been in the hundreds. Some records show that the group knew an aerosolized attack would be more effective but they either could not work out a reliable, portable delivery device or they deliberately chose a less lethal method. Either way, the attack was successful and terrifying.
>
> Even with this inefficient delivery method, the attack sickened hundreds of people and terrified thousands. Of the 5,000 people that were seen and treated at a hospital, only about 800 were transported by ambulance. The remainder all self-transported to any medical facility, terrified that they had been exposed and were going to fall ill at any moment. Many of these individuals had been in or near the subway system but were not exposed to the agent; they were perfectly healthy, but scared. This is the classic example of how a small event can trigger a flood of **"worried-well"** that must be dealt with, but can overwhelm and flood limited response resources.

Neurotoxins can be synthesized from commercial chemicals by a competent chemist. That should not be taken to mean that making them is "easy," but only that it is possible. Further, some organophosphate fertilizers can be used as crude nerve agents, though they will lack the potency of weaponized material.

Chemical Asphyxiates

Chemical asphyxiates are poisons that are absorbed into the blood, and include the well-known **cyanide** family. This class of chemical prevents the cells in the body from absorbing or using oxygen, which causes those cells to die. This effect is amplified in the brain and the lungs, where cells require large amounts of oxygen to function. These chemicals are often used in industrial applications, or are by products of industrial processes.

Hydrogen cyanide, which is also known by the military designation AC, is a colorless gas, and is simple to deliver using artillery shells, spray tanks, and other devices. Some people report the gas has a slight smell of almonds, but not everyone can detect this smell. The most dangerous exposure method is inhalation, although it can be toxic if ingested in sufficient quantities. Cyanide gas is less dense than air so it will rise after release. When this is combined with a rapid evaporation rate, these weapons are most effective in enclosed or indoor spaces.

Respiratory Irritants

Respiratory irritants cause severe inflammation of the respiratory tract, including the nose, throat, and lungs. They are common in industrial and household applications making them simple to acquire. These agents can be fatal, but primarily cause debilitating injury to exposed individuals. Two of the most common respiratory irritants, chlorine and phosgene, were used as chemical weapons in WWI.

Chlorine is a common industrial chemical that is in gas form at typical "room temperature" and pressure. It can be pressurized into a liquid state in a container, but when the container is opened, the liquid will quickly convert back to a gaseous state. Chlorine is used in the manufacture of paper and cloth, in household cleaners, and in water purification systems and is commonly manufactured and transported in the United States.

Chlorine gas has a higher density than air, which means it will stay low to the ground, and has a strong pungent bleach-like odor. In low wind conditions, pockets of chlorine gas may stay in low-lying areas long after release and the agent can persist indoors or in an enclosed space for a long time.

Symptoms of chlorine exposure include coughing, a burning sensation in the nose, eyes and throat, watery or blurred vision, blistered or irritated skin, shortness of breath, and fluid in the lungs. These symptoms may appear immediately upon exposure and develop and worsen as time progresses.

Phosgene is also a gas at typical room temperature and pressure and can be pressurized into liquid form for transport. Like chlorine, phosgene will quickly expand from liquid to gas upon release and has an odor that is described as similar to freshly cut grass. Victims can be exposed to phosgene gas through inhalation as well as skin and eye contact. In liquid form, phosgene can be introduced through water, either by drinking it or coming into contact with the contaminated water.

The symptoms for phosgene poisoning are very similar to those of chlorine poisoning. However, phosgene victims can show a secondary set of symptoms up to 48 hours after exposure, including difficulty breathing, low blood pressure, and heart failure. For these reasons, phosgene gas is regarded as the most deadly of all the chemical agents used in WWI.

Skin Irritants

Skin irritants or **vesicants** are a class of chemical agent designed to cause blistering of the skin and mucous membranes including eyes, nose, and lungs. They are painful, crippling agents but are often not fatal. The most famous skin irritant is sulfur mustard, commonly referred to as mustard gas. Mustard gas killed fewer than 5% of soldiers exposed to it, but it was extremely effective in crippling exposed units and rendering them unable to fight. Soldiers were often blinded, which required relatively healthy troops to assist them to safety. Mustard gas was also a potent psychological weapon. It would often take two to four hours for symptoms to appear, and the characteristic smell of onions or garlic was not always present. This meant that soldiers lived in fear of a gas attack that could overcome them without warning or recourse—by the time symptoms appeared, exposure was complete.

Sulfur mustard is an oily-textured liquid, either clear or yellowish brown in color. It was typically delivered in gas form, often from barrels placed upwind of the target area. It is denser than air, so it stays low to the ground, and it can be carried miles by the wind. Symptoms of sulfur mustard exposure include redness and irritation of the skin, pain and swelling in the eyes, light sensitivity in the eyes, temporary blindness, runny nose, bloody nose, shortness of breath, and coughing.

Other skin irritants include Lewisite, which was created at the end of WWI but saw no wartime use. It was similar to sulfur mustard, but acted immediately on contact.

Anti-personnel Agents

Anti-personnel agents are nonlethal chemicals designed to cause irritation and discomfort for crowd and riot control. Examples of these chemicals include tear gas (military designation CS) and pepper spray.

These agents are considered "safe" for military and law enforcement use, but are included here for one primary reason: They may be employed by terrorists as a coercive weapon or tactic. These agents are easy to obtain in most states in the United States and are legal to posses in many jurisdictions.

Biological Weapons

Biological weapons are defined as utilizing biological toxins or infectious agents to incapacitate or kill. These agents may include living organisms or entities that replicate and live inside a host victim. Biological weapons have existed in warfare for hundreds of years, and reports of armies using dead animals to poison wells and water sources go back almost 2,000 years. Western settlers gave blankets infected with smallpox to Native Americans, waging indiscriminate biological warfare on entire societies. In modern-day Oregon, a cult used salmonella to poison the residents of a small town, hoping to influence a local election.

Biological weapons are common, they are cheap to produce, and while their effectiveness is at the mercy of many factors, they are certainly terrifying. These factors combine to create a large potential for future terrorist use.

Unlike chemical weapons, the time between exposure to the weapons and the onset of symptoms can be quite long, often days or even weeks. This delayed onset makes it very difficult to detect exactly when and where a biological attack occurred. Further, many biological agents are naturally occurring diseases or toxins. An attack may go undetected until a significant (and unusual) number of cases appear in a geographic location. All of these factors make it possible for a terrorist to design an attack and be gone from the target area for days or weeks before authorities and the public even know an event is underway.

Chemical weapons typically require direct exposure to the agent. The victim must be in the area where phosgene or VX are deployed, and must come into contact with the chemical. That is not true with biological weapons. A victim infected with a bacteria or virus may be **contagious**, spreading the disease to new victims as they go to school, shop for groceries, or eat in a restaurant. One victim can become 10, who in turn become 10 more, exponentially increasing the exposed victim count. As a biological weapon spreads on its own, it becomes a **contagion**.

These factors alone make biological agents effective terrorist weapons—but there is more. You cannot see, smell, or taste these agents; they are undetectable by the human senses. Many biological agents are hundreds of times more toxic than a chemical weapon; botulinum is 15,000 times more toxic than Sarin (a chemical nerve gas). When all of these attributes are weighed, these weapons are guaranteed to strike fear into a victim population.

There are three types of biological weapon: bacteria, virus, and toxin. Let's look at each.

Bacteria

Bacteria are unicellular microorganisms and exist practically everywhere in nature, including inside the human body. They reproduce through fission, where one bacteria splits and becomes two. Don't confuse this with nuclear fission, which we will discuss later. The majority of bacteria are harmless (or even useful or necessary) to humans, but a few can cause illness and are suitable for use as a weapon. We will look at one example of these agents in detail—anthrax.

Anthrax, formally known as *Bacillus anthracis*, is naturally occurring, and can be found in the soil and around hoofed animals such as cattle and sheep. It can form spores that help protect the bacteria from the environment and allow it to lie dormant for long periods of time. It is not uncommon to see a naturally occurring anthrax infection in rural areas of the western United States.

Anthrax can infect humans in three ways. The most common (naturally) is *cutaneous*—an infection of the skin. This occurs when the bacteria enters a break in the skin, usually a cut or scrape, and infects the underlying tissue. This form of infection, called cutaneous anthrax infection, is highly treatable with antibiotics and has a survival rate of well over 99%.

Gastrointestinal (GI) anthrax infection occurs when bacteria is consumed, typically in undercooked or raw meat from infected animals. This form of infection is very dangerous, but is the most rare of the anthrax infections; there have been no cases of GI anthrax reported inside the United States. Symptoms of GI anthrax include classic flu-like symptoms such as high fever and fatigue, nausea, vomiting, diarrhea, sore throat or neck, and difficulty swallowing. These symptoms typically appear one to seven days after ingestion of the bacteria, and the disease is fatal in 25 to 60% of cases.

The most severe form of anthrax infection is *inhalational* anthrax. In these cases, anthrax spores are inhaled by the victim and come to rest in the lungs and mucous membranes. Symptoms often resemble a common cold and include a mild fever and sore throat. These mild symptoms progress to more severe problems, including cough, chest pain, high fever, and difficulty swallowing. Inhalational anthrax is usually fatal, even with antibiotic treatment.

Sverdlovsk Incident

In early April 1979, an accidental release of anthrax spores occurred at a microbiological military facility in Sverdlovsk, in the former Soviet Union. The release consisted of weaponized spores intended to be delivered in an aerosol format.

The purpose of this facility was to mill anthrax into a weaponized form and fill warheads and other munitions with the agent. While the dayshift workers were drying milled anthrax and making it into a powder, they discovered that the safety air filters for the room had become clogged. These filters were removed for replacement, but the next shift of workers failed to replace them. This allowed milled anthrax spores to be blown through the ventilation system and into the outside air.

Within 10 days, residents living downwind from the compound developed high fevers and difficulty breathing, and at least 66 people died. Although the Soviets blamed the deaths on the consumption of contaminated meat, most experts at the time suspected that these fatalities were from inhaling aerosolized anthrax released from the manufacturing facility. These facts were confirmed in 1992 when Russian President Boris Yeltsin acknowledged the accident and the subsequent release of weaponized anthrax into the local environment.

Anthrax spores are too small to be seen with the naked eye and have no distinctive smell or taste. Infections are not considered to be contagious; in this manner anthrax behaves much like a chemical weapon. Inhalational anthrax seldom occurs naturally. While the spores are too small to be seen, when they occur in nature, they are too large to remain suspended in the air for any significant time. **Weaponized anthrax** consists of anthrax spores that have been milled or ground to a uniform consistency. This powder is very fine and can be aerosolized much like a chemical agent. Once released into the air, it can carry for a long distance on prevailing winds; this attribute makes it an ideal biological weapon.

In 2001, seven letters were mailed to a variety of media organizations and elected officials. These letters contained highly refined anthrax spores, which sickened 22 people and killed five. There have been a variety of hypothesis put forward by law enforcement and the media as to the source and motive of the attacks, but nothing concrete has been determined; the *"Amerithrax"* attacks are still unsolved.

There are other bacteria that are usable as biological agents, but none of these has been developed so completely as a weapon. Bacteria can be treated with antibiotics such as amoxicillin and penicillin to varying degrees of effectiveness. Some, such as inhalational anthrax, are dangerous even with treatment, while others, such as salmonella, can be cured with an appropriate course of drugs. Only bacteria can be treated in this way; antibiotics are useless versus a virus.

Virus

A **virus** is a microscopic organism and infectious agent that replicates itself inside of a host victim. Unlike bacteria, which can grow in many places, a virus requires a living host, but it can reproduce at alarming rates. Viral diseases are common in our society and include influenza and the common cold. Not all viruses are biological weapons, or would be suitable for such, and even the mundane agents such as influenza are fatal to thousands of people each year in the United States—just from naturally occurring infections.

As we discussed before, viruses are not affected by antibiotics. Further, most viral infections are contagious, often before a person even knows he or she is infected. Let's use influenza as an example. An infected person is contagious and actively spreading virus-laden vapor with every breath, cough, and sneeze within hours of initial infection. This is before the victim begins to feel sick and show significant symptoms. This lag time enables an infected person who is traveling in public to infect dozens of other people, who will in turn infect dozens more and so on. This contagion effect could create a dangerous biological weapon. Some planners worry about the "bio martyr," a person who is knowingly infected with a dangerous or deadly virus so he or she can carry it into a population. These individuals would be difficult to detect and stop, and a potent virus could spread quickly.

The most common viral weapon, in current planning scenarios, is smallpox or the *Variola* virus. Eradicated in the wild since 1980, smallpox is a highly contagious virus that causes fever, vomiting, headache, backache, and a distinctive rash and legions. While there is a vaccine for smallpox, it has not been routinely used in the United States since the early 1980s (remember, the disease is eradicated) and current supplies are limited. The lesions and rash are horrifying and frightening, and smallpox is fatal in approximately 30% of cases. The Soviet Union had a smallpox weaponization program, and the Unites States and other nations have considerable stockpiles of the virus for research purposes.

Another "doomsday' example is **viral hemorrhagic fever** (VHF)—producing agents. First, remember that VHF is not a virus, but the dramatic symptom of many different types of viruses, the most famous of which are Ebola and Marburg. The viruses that cause VHF are zoonotic in nature: They naturally reside in the animal population but under certain circumstances can infect humans. Once in a human host, these viruses are often dangerously contagious and can spread through contact with infected material such as blood or other bodily secretions. VHF is often fatal, causing profuse and horrifying bleeding internally, under the skin, and from eyes, nose, mouth, and other orifices (the hemorrhaging) as well as fever, nausea, vomiting, and diarrhea.

Ebola, Marburg, and other VHF-producing viruses are often discussed as potential biological weapons, but they suffer from several drawbacks. First, they cause symptoms to appear very quickly. This limits that time after infection when a person can spread the disease without knowing he or she is sick. Further, human-to-human transmission is not as easy as it is with influenza, where the disease can become airborne on sneezes and coughs. Last, the symptoms of these diseases are truly terrifying. While influenza may manifest as a cough or a cold, VHF is a dramatic disease and people instinctively know that something very, very bad is happening and seek treatment. In other words, an influenza victim may continue about his or her normal activities for a while, but a Marburg victim seeks medical treatment quickly and is therefore isolated form the rest of the population. Put simply, VHF agents are too frightening a weapon to spread much.

Finally, the VHF agents have high fatality rates, with some approaching 90%. When you combine rapid onset, frightening visible symptoms, and high death rate, you get a disease with a very high "burn rate." It can and will kill many infected people, but it can be caught and controlled. In other words, Ebola is not going to destroy the entire population of the United States, Florida, or even a large city. Natural outbreaks in Africa produce death tolls measured in the hundreds, not hundreds of thousands.

All that said, a VHF virus would be a frightening biological weapons and attractive to terrorists. The Soviet Union biological weapons program was attempting to weaponize Marburg as late as 1990, and even fictionalized accounts of these types of weapons have driven the creation of policy here in the United States (Public Broadcasting Corporation, 2001).

Toxins

The last category of biological weapon is **toxins**. These are not contagious at all and act very much like potent chemical weapons requiring direct exposure to the agent. Toxins are naturally occurring, but several have been determined to be acceptable for use a biological weapons.

Botulinum is a neurotoxin (attacks the nervous system of the victim) that is fast acting and causes mental confusion, motor control and balance issues, vision problems, tremors, and seizures. Botulinum is the most lethal material on the planet by weight and is approximately 15,000 times more toxic than the chemical agent VX.

When ingested, botulinum causes the disease botulism. This can occur naturally with improperly or contaminated canned foods and is a painful and dangerous form of food poisoning. Botulinum can also be aerosolized, but it less effective in this manner.

Ricin is a cytotoxin (attacks the victim's cells), which is slower acting and produces symptoms such as vomiting, diarrhea, jaundice, rashes or blisters, and general tissue deterioration. Ricin is about 10 times more toxic than the chemical nerve agent Sarin and is derived from the castor bean. It is usually ingested to cause sickness but can also be injected into the victim. Ricin poisoning is typically fatal in untreated cases.

Not So Fast

These descriptions are frightening to read and can easily be stretched into doomsday scenarios. The reality is that these kinds of weapons are not that easy to use.

Both chemical and biological weapons could be used by a terrorist organization to kill or sicken dozens if not hundreds of people. However, in many cases, greater casualties could be caused by an improvised explosive device. It is usually simpler to use an explosive in most scenarios as well.

Both chemical and biological weapon effectiveness (the ability to cause harm) can be impacted by the environment. Temperature, wind, humidity, precipitation etc. can limit or destroy the ability of these agents to harm or kill. Viruses often require populations to be in close contact for the contagious effect to cause spread of the disease.

Let's look at some examples. Remember the Amerithrax attacks described a few pages back? The two letters that were mailed to Senators Leahy and Dashle each contained approximately 1 gram of milled, weaponized anthrax with enough spores to infect and kill almost 100 million people. Put another way, there were enough spores in all of the envelopes to kill the entire population of the United States. The attack killed five. This illustrates the fact that biological weapons are hard to manufacture and handle, and they are hard to distribute effectively.

Aum Shrinko is best known for the 1995 Tokyo subway Sarin attack. This was a crude but effective use of a chemical weapon, but it was not their first attempt. Years before the 1995 attack, they equipped trucks with pressurized tanks and spray valves, loaded these with botulinum and drove through Tokyo, spraying the deadly toxin in the air. No one noticed. When that didn't work, the cult aerosolized anthrax and sprayed it from their trucks as well as from tanks on Tokyo rooftops. Again, no one noticed.

These examples illustrate the difficulty in using biological weapons. In these examples, we assume that the agents used were viable, but that the delivery failed. This could be because of incorrect agent concentrations, environmental factors such as the wind, temperature, or humidity, or faulty delivery devices. Even if a terrorist organization has the capacity to produce a biological weapon (and that is no small feat), that does not translate to an instantly effective weapon.

Radiological Devices

Imagine an explosion on a busy street. The blast kills and wounds dozens, creating instant chaos and confusion. Unknown to the victims and survivors, the entire street is now under threat from a cloud of invisible radioactive particles. These are inhaled, ingested, and coat the clothing, hair, and skin of even those who escaped the initial blast. The particles are inside vehicles, pulled into building ventilation systems, and deposited throughout the area. This invisible threat emits dangerous and potentially deadly radiation and could sicken or kill hundreds of victims days after the blast.

This is the threat scenario for a **radiological dispersal device** or RDD. These "dirty bombs" are conventional explosives that scatter a radioactive isotope throughout the blast area. These radioactive agents can cause illness and death, as well as create massive economic damage from the resulting cleanup and restoration of the area. In most cases, the initial explosion of the conventional bomb will create more casualties that the following radiological casualties, but the invisible and insidious nature of the attack amplifies the fear and terror of the population.

There are several materials that would be suitable for use in an RDD, and some of these can be found in most cities in the United States. Medical waste, by-products of manufacturing, and other processes can create a radiological material ready to use in an RDD. These materials are tracked closely, but it is possible for them to fall into the wrong hands.

I want to point out something that is very important. In no way is an RDD a nuclear device. There is no fission or fusion reaction; no nuclear detonation. People tend to confuse the two because both are radioactive, but they are very different in concept and effect.

Nuclear Weapons

Finally, let's talk about the only true weapon of mass destruction. I mean that, the other WMDs we discuss here are junior partners in this arrangement. None of them, none, can bring about the violent and widespread damage and destruction of a nuclear weapon. Does that make the others less attractive to terrorists? No.

The reality is, while a nuke would cause the most destruction and terror, it is also the hardest to acquire or construct. We should all be happy about that.

The first nuclear detonation occurred on July 16, 1945, in the desert of New Mexico. Less than one month later, the United States dropped two nuclear devices on the Japanese cities of Hiroshima (August 6) and Nagasaki (August 9). These attacks resulted in almost 150,000 deaths (more would come from radiation, reaching over 300,000 by 1950) and the surrender of Japan at the end of World War II. These two detonations are the only times in human history that nuclear weapons have been used in war. Most people hope they are the last, but we are not going to bet on that (Federation of American Scientists, 1998).

The weapons employed for the United States in that fateful August are crude by later standards; modern weapons are capable of even more destruction. "Little Boy," the uranium-based weapon dropped on Hiroshima, yielded the equivalent of 16 kilotons of TNT—about 35 million pounds. The more advanced, plutonium-based "Fat Man" weapon that was dropped on Nagasaki yielded 21 kilotons. For comparison, a modern U.S. sea-launched ballistic missile (SLBM) fired from a ballistic missile submarine can carry four (4) independent 475kt weapons (Federation of American Scientists, 1998; U.S. Nuclear Regulatory Commission, 2003).

We could write an entire chapter (or even an entire textbook) on nuclear weapons. For our purposes, we don't need as much detail. The basics are simple—and the basics are what we face from a terrorist organization.

To create a nuclear weapon, an organization would need a sufficient quantity of one of two **fissionable** materials—**highly enriched uranium (HEU)** or **plutonium-239**. HEU consists of a composite of different uranium isotopes, with at least 20% of the mass being the uranium-235 isotope. At 20% concentration of uranium-235, the material is considered "weapons usable" and would be sufficient for a crude, low yield weapon. At the 80% uranium-235 threshold, the material becomes "weapons-grade" and would produce a high-yield explosion. HEU does not exist in nature and requires significant engineering capability to produce from typical (naturally occurring) uranium. The isotope plutonium-239 is the second fissionable material and also does not occur in nature. In fact, plutonium-239 is the byproduct of breeder nuclear reactors—you have to have an existing nuclear capability to create this material (U.S. Nuclear Regulatory Commission, 2003).

From a terrorist perspective, it would be difficult to produce either of these required materials; it is much more feasible to steal or purchase them. Even better would be to acquire an intact and functional weapon.

To be clear, a terrorist nuclear weapon is a worst-case scenario. Even a crude weapon constructed from existing engineering plans with manufactured or acquired fissionable material could yield 10 kilotons—enough to destroy a significant portion of Lower Manhattan. This assumes the weapon is delivered by truck and detonated on the street, the most likely terrorist use case scenario. We can extrapolate increased damage from larger weapons, but the probability of these being used by a terrorist organization is low.

We cannot assume that every terrorist organization would want to acquire or use a nuclear weapon (or other CBRN weapon, for that matter). The current and highly visible trend in terrorism involves organizations such as al Qaeda, who embrace a nearly apocalyptical view of terrorism and are willing to inflict massive casualties and destruction (witness 9/11). These religious terrorists have stepped away from the model from pervious decades, where small, controlled events were used to amplify a grievance or dispute, and mass casualties were not the goal. These more traditional model terrorists understood that while violence was necessary, it should be carefully directed and controlled, less they risk losing the support of their constituent populations. The usage of a nuclear weapon (or other WMD) goes against that tenet and would be counterproductive.

That said, al Qaeda or another organization of that type may employ a nuclear weapon if it can acquire one. Our best defense against this is watchful monitoring of existing weapons and fissionable materials, combined with diplomacy and other action to prevent further proliferation of the technology. Al Qaeda and its allies do not possess the engineering capacity to construct a weapon, even if they possess fissionable material, so we need to make sure they do not acquire one from existing sources.

Our biggest threat in this area comes from Iran, who is still actively attempting to build a nuclear program. If Iran succeeds in building a weapon, it is not beyond reason that the device could wind up in the hands of Hezbollah for use against Israel or the West. Fortunately for us, Iran recognizes that such a use of a nuclear weapon would instantly be attributed to them, and they are not a suicidal nation. The swift and terrible capacity for retribution against Iran for such an action will serve to deter them from that course. We hope.

Technical/Cyber

The last category of WMD, only occasionally used professionally, is the technical or cyber weapons. I'll make this section very simple—these weapons and tactics do not exist. Yet. It is possible that at some point in our future we will see a cyber capability that progresses to the point of being considered a WMD, but that weapon is fiction today.

The modern media (and government planners) love to talk about cyberterrorism and the chaos it could cause. And while cybercrime is increasing and a real threat to our infrastructure, transportation and financial systems, cyberterrorism has yet to manifest itself. Similarly, the doomsday cyberweapon has yet to develop and is certainly not in the same category as a nuclear weapon—or even a chemical, biological, or radiological weapon.

Key Terms

Aerosol	Plutonium-239
Ammonium nitrate and fuel oil (ANFO)	Radiological dispersal device
Bacteria	Respiratory irritants
Biological weapons	Rifles
CBRN	Rocket or Rocket propelled grenade
Chemical weapons	(RPG)
Chemical asphyxiates	Semtex
Contagion	Shrapnel
Contagious	Shotguns
Conventional weapons	Skin irritants
Cyanide	Submachine guns
Fissionable	Threat weapon
Fuse	Timers
Gasoline or alcohol bomb	Toxin
Hand grenades	Trigger device
Handguns	Vesicants
Highly enriched uranium	Virus
Machine guns	Viral hemorrhagic fever
Molotov cocktail	Weapon of mass destruction
Neurotoxins	Weaponized anthrax
Precursor materials	Worried-well

Discussion Questions

1. If a modern, religious terrorist organization acquires a weapon of mass destruction, will it use it? Why or why not?

2. Why has the United States put such a great focus on terrorism involving weapons of mass destruction? Is this good policy or bad?

References

Federation of American Scientists. (1998, May 1). *Trident II D-5 Fleet Ballistic Missile*. Retrieved February 5, 2013, from Federation of American Scientists: www.fas.org/nuke/guide/usa/slbm/d-5.htm

Public Broadasting Corporation. (2001, November 1). *Interviews with Biowarriors: Bill Patrick*. Retrieved February 2, 2013, from Nova Online: www.pbs.org/wgbh/nova/bioterror/biow_patrick.html

U.S. Nuclear Regulatory Commission. (2003, October 1). *Fact Sheet on Plutonium*. Retrieved Febraury 5, 2013, from U.S. Nuclear Regulatory Commission: www.nrc.gov/reading-rm/doc-collections/fact-sheets/plutonium.html

Walker, G. (2005, March 1). *The First Atomic Test*. Retrieved February 3, 2013, from Trinity Atomic Web Site: www.cddc.vt.edu/host/atomic/trinity/trinity1.htm

Chapter 6

Pseudo-Terrorism

A s was mentioned before, it's entirely possible there is no such thing as terrorism. If you look at the previous definition, the common attribute is to threaten or coerce a population with violence. But think about that—isn't violence by its very nature threating? What if everything we consider terrorism really just falls out on a spectrum of violence starting with criminal actions, conducted at the individual level and escalating to full-scale war, conducted between states, at the other end?

Our goal is not to confuse you, but to give you tools to defend your thinking and help you be the smartest person in the room! Along those lines there are several "types" of terrorism whose definitions are inherently conflictual and should not be labeled as terrorism.

Criminal Terrorism

This term has been used occasionally, probably as a way to draw on resources from the global war on terror for other initiatives undertaken by law enforcement organizations. It alludes to the use of extraordinary violence to threaten or influence an audience *in the furtherance of a crime.* While almost all crime feels threatening and intimidating, the users of this term were probably referring specifically to "organized crime." Within criminal activities there is a spectrum of organization ranging from an individual criminal motivated by personal gain to a large centralized criminal enterprise that engages in illegal activities for profit. Organized criminals are best known as perpetrators of racketeering—the extortion of money to solve a problem that may not exist or is actually created by the criminal enterprise itself.

It is important to distinguish from the beginning that crime and political violence differ at their very root; crimes are conducted for personal profit, and terrorism is committed in the name of a cause. The foundational difference in motivation and gain between terrorism and crime creates the inherent conflict it the term *criminal terrorism*.

"Wait?" you say, "Isn't terrorism a crime and isn't crime terrifying?" While your statement embraces the obvious, the first problem is not all crimes are terrifying. Many crimes (money laundering, illegal gambling, prostitution, public displays of drunkenness, etc.) are distressing, unfortunate, or gross—but not terrifying. Few of us lay awake at night "terrified" of international banking fraud or college students puking on sidewalks.

© photo.ua, 2013. Used under license from Shuttershock, Inc.

"Within crime there is a spectrum of organization"

Alternately, the presence of criminality is implied in the term *terrorism*. Many definitions of terrorism include the details of the criminal activity; "destructions of property," "violence against innocents," but the illegal component of the actions is part of what makes the word terrorism unique. If we mention "peaceful terrorism," the oxymoron is obvious because terrorism is by nature violent and criminal.

It is important to also explore the motivation for what is terrorism and why people commit acts of such extraordinary violence. The motivation of terrorists is rarely for personal gain or profit. Criminals, on the other hand, are very motivated by personal profit and are also focused on their safety and escape route. If you look at the table below, you can see the different motivational attributes of both terrorists and criminals.

Criminals	Terrorists
Motivated by greed or personal gain	Motivated by cause and beliefs
Escape is a priority	Cause is greater than the self
Activities are secret	Publicity is part of the plan
Individually focused	Part of a larger movement
Victims are opportunity based	Victims are symbolic

When compared side by side, criminal enterprise and terrorism could not be more different. The motivations are different (profit vs. cause), the actors are different (escape oriented vs. willing to die for the cause), the laws used to prosecute who we catch in the act are different (USA PATRIOT ACT vs. RICO) and finally the courts are different—notably we have no international court of terrorism.

Military Dissident Terrorism

When violent political acts are conducted by a non-state, uniform-wearing organization, we already have a name for them—**guerillas**. The term *guerilla* comes from the Spanish meaning "little war," and guerilla fighters are often found in very specific circumstances. First, because guerilla forces wear uniforms and insignia, they are considered a *bright* or *open network;* you only have to look at their lapels to see what their position is in the organization.

Military dissident groups can also be called **paramilitary** organizations, which may be similar to regular or professional militaries, but are not formally part of any state or country. There are also **militias,** which are another type of armed force, usually comprised of non-professional fighters who as civilians may pick up arms to supplement state militaries.

Terror organizations are often called **dark networks** because it is difficult to openly see the relationship between members of the organization. **Bright networks,** by contrast, allow the bystander or observer to know who is in an organization and where his or her position in the chain of command is. One of the best examples of a bright network can be found in militaries, especially in the U.S. military. If you see a soldier from the U.S. armed forces, you will see several things denoting her exact position within the organization. First, you will know what branch she is in—Army, Air Force, Navy, Marines, or Coast Guard—by the unique cut and color of her apparel. Second, you will know the soldier's name, which is worn on her uniform for all to see. Third, you will know a soldier's rank, indicating exactly where in the organization that soldier is located, providing information about who she reports to, and who reports to her. Rank may also offer indications of how long that soldier has served in that branch. Fourth, a patch worn on the shoulder may indicate which unit that solder is assigned to or serving in. Last, you may see tabs, devices, or medals indicating special skill sets the soldier has, including Ranger Force, Air Assault (with jumps), Paratrooper, Pathfinder, etc. All of this organizational information is worn on the casual everyday uniform, providing a great deal of information about any soldier. If you get to observe U.S. soldiers in their dress uniforms, you will be able to tell which campaigns the soldier has deployed on, including where and how many times, which schools or training they've gone to, and myriad other career details. Compare this to a stranger in a café, and you can see why the armed forces are one of the brightest network organizations in the world.

Another unique characteristic of guerillas is that they are often focused on a specific geographical region, where they *seize and hold territory*. The geopolitical focus on land and its governance is one of the unique characteristics of guerilla forces, and guerillas are usually specifically focused on the situation in the country they are located. Unlike other global terror networks or global causes, guerilla groups are focused on the governance and control of their own land. The guerilla focus on the geopolitical also means they are rarely religious or cause based and do not seek to change the circumstances outside their own country. For example, the Tamil Tigers of Sri Lanka did not focus on the geopolitics of South America. Conversely, the Shining Path (Sendero Lumnioso), a Maoist guerilla group in Peru never used a struggle on the other side of the world as a reason for their existence.

Another example of **military dissident terrorism** can be found when a faction of a country's regular armed forces breaks off and tries to overthrow the government. This is usually referred to as a *military coup d'etat* or *coup*. If the military coup succeeds and overthrows the government, then this is sometimes called a *military revolution*, or *military overthrow*. In 2009 the Honduran army seized a presidential palace and kidnapped then-President Zelaya, subsequently exiling him Costa Rica while he was voted out of office. In this Honduran example, the military coup was supported by the Honduran congress and resulted in a peaceful, although legally unusual, change of government. However, when a military coup fails, the unfortunate participants are labeled "deserters" or "seditious" (acting against your own country) and often killed as punishment.

Narcoterrorism

The term ***narcoterrorism*** was coined by President Terry of Peru in the 1980s to describe the violence surrounding the drug trade. The term *narcoterrorism* was meant to draw attention to the extraordinary violence, intimidation, and extortion the drug cartels were using on citizens and governments in South America. While drug cartels are considered criminal enterprises, the term *narcoterrorism* was meant to describe the violence specific to the drug trade.

The term *narcoterrorism* was never intended to reflect the cause-based initiatives in most terror groups, and a more contemporary description would be "drug-associated violence." The classic example of this type of violence was found in Pablo Escobar's ruthless dealings in Colombia as part of the cocaine trade. Escobar routinely bribed or killed hundreds, if not thousands, of politicians, policemen, and civilians as part of his cocaine trafficking enterprise. (Escobar was famous for his "*plata o plomo*" offer—literally the choice between silver (bribes) or lead (death).) Escobar's international criminal enterprise was clearly profit motivated and sought only personal gain.

With the introduction of the "War on Drugs" campaign undertaken by the United States starting in 1971, the term *narcoterrorism* became politicized. Using military forces to reduce the production and distribution of illegal drugs has proved costly and counterproductive, and recently both the term *narcoterrorism* and the "War on Drugs" have been dropped from the federal lexicon.

And Then There Was FARC: A Case Study on the Evolution of a Group

The Revolutionary Armed Forces of Colombia—Peoples Army (Fuerzas Armadas Revolucionarias de Colombia—Ejército del Pueblo), or FARC-EP, is one of the oldest continuously active terrorist organizations in the world. **FARC** has a long and complicated evolution, and its origins can be found in the Colombian Communist Party (Partido Comunista Colombiano) or PCC organized in the years following World War I. As part of a global movement embracing Marxist-Leninist leanings, the PCC organized peasants and laborers in rural Colombia, calling for improved working and living conditions and access to education. Recognized as a political party in 1930, the PCC organized strikes and protests that drew violent attention from the Colombian central government. During the Colombian Civil War from 1948–1958, known as La Violencia, many members of the PCC were targeted by the Colombian government for their political affiliation, and an estimated 300,000 Colombians were killed.

After La Violencia, in the 1960s the Colombian government introduced a policy of Accelerated Economic Development (AED) that promoted industrial farming, often evicting families from their lands. This became a focusing event for many rural peasants and laborers and in an effort to resist the Colombian seizure of land, members of the PCC formed an armed resistance group which became FARC-EP in 1964.[1]

The mission of FARC during its founding was to defend the poor and fight the perceived imperialists and agri-capitalists in Colombia, while embracing the Bolivarianism philosophy of democratic socialism. (Bolivarianism is based on the political thinking of Simon Bolivar and includes both democratic processes and socialist ideologies.) Because FARC considered itself an armed resistance group, members organized and wore the uniforms of a paramilitary or guerrilla group and were able to resist Colombian military advances in southern Colombia.

FARC enjoyed moderate success in southern Colombia throughout the 1970s and continued to draw attention to the rural poor they were championing. However, running out of funding, FARC became involved in the booming drug trade of the mid 1970–1980s, exchanging protection of the cartels for weapons and money. This shift in allegiances changed both the capacity and the mission of FARC, dramatically changing how they would fight and be perceived. The increased weaponry and financing allowed FARC to bring its fight closer to the capital, and with bigger weapons, they led several large-scale attacks on the Colombian military in the early 1980s. With the increased funding, FARC was also able to send fighters to the Soviet Union and Vietnam for advanced tactics training. Interestingly, these tactics worked, and in 1984 the Colombian president began peace talks with the FARC guerillas, resulting in the La Uribe Agreement cease fire that lasted until 1987.

---

[1] Some documents use the date of 1966 as the year FARC became a formal guerilla group, as opposed to the 1964 PCC/FARC splinter date.

The reasons for the break in the ceasefire are many and include the central government's insistence that FARC was not maintaining its end of the agreement. During this period FARC was by all accounts heavily involved in the drug trade, and Colombian drug syndicates like Pablo Escobar's Medellin cartel hired FARC to protect its crops, workers, and processing plants. This affiliation with the drug cartels, and the exploitation of the very peasants and laborers FARC was founded to protect, changed the perception and the purpose of the group.

In 1999 the Colombian government made an extraordinary effort to bring peace and a ceasefire with FARC. In a land-for-peace deal, Colombia offered 16,000 square miles of land to FARC in the southern region, an area the size of Switzerland. Under this agreement FARC could live and govern as it saw fit, in essence creating a Bolivarianism state within Colombia. FARC already controlled most of this land, which was being used for coca (cocaine) farms, but the peace agreement would keep Colombian and U.S. militaries out of the area. Unbelievably, FARC did not comply with the peace accord and in 1999 killed three U.S. aid workers who were assisting indigenous peoples in Colombia, drawing international condemnation for FARC and increasing pressure on Colombia to eliminate FARC.

From 2001–2006 the Office of the U.S. Attorney General announced indictments for the leaders of FARC for international drug trafficking charges. A single 2006 indictment identified 50 leaders of FARC responsible for bringing in $25 *billion* dollars' worth of cocaine into the United States. More recently, several leaders of FARC have appeared on the Justice Department's Consolidated Priority Organization target list, which identifies the most dangerous international drug traffickers, and additional indictments were served to affiliates who provided military-grade weapons to FARC.

No longer considered freedom fighters for the people, but rather puppets of the drug trade, FARC does not enjoy the popular rural support it once had. In 2005 the United Nations Commission on Human Rights condemned FARC for gross human rights violations, including torture and kidnapping, of civilian men, women, and children, including protected ethnic groups. By 2008 popular disillusion with FARC came to a head and anti-FARC protests, organized via social media with hundreds of thousands of participants, were held throughout Colombia.

In 2013 FARC and representatives of the Colombian government met in Cuba to discuss a peace agreement that could end the half century of conflict. FARC continues to demand land reforms and a legitimate place in the political process, but Colombian officials are wary of the group's ability to extract itself from the drug enterprise it has become synonymous with.

While it is unclear what the eventual resolution of this conflict will be, what makes FARC fascinating is the changes it has gone through in its 50 years as a terrorist organization. Looking at the origins of the group as an offshoot of the communist PCC movement, in the 1960s FARC was a group focused on a cause, specifically land rights and equality for the poor. The FARC splintering away from the PCC to pursue a more violent agenda clearly follows the Moghaddam staircase model presented in Chapter 2. What made FARC unique at the time was its adaptation of the paramilitary/guerilla organizational structure, including the wearing of uniforms, making them a covert but bright network.

In spite of repeatedly offered peace deals that *included land,* which it could govern according to its own beliefs, FARC broke multiple peace accords in favor of a criminal relationship that offered financing. To state it crudely, FARC turned its back on its cause in the name of making money and changed a once ideologically based organization into a criminal enterprise.

While the relationship between criminal enterprises and terrorist organization is prolific, what makes FARC unique is its deep association and support of a specific enterprise (drug trafficking) that eventually lost it supporters. In essence, a once cause-based group of Robin Hood–like fighters became the henchmen of the world's most notorious drug cartel, killing in the name of greed. This is a stunning evolution for a terrorist organization, and FARC is considered unique in terrorism studies.

Cyberterrorism

Cyberterrorism is a complicated and contentious issue, further exacerbated by our need to call everything terrorism. There are several criteria that have to be included in any definition of terrorism, and one of the most important is extraordinary violence or the threat of extraordinary violence for the purpose of intimidation or coercion. The conjoining of violence and purpose are the core of what makes terrorism a unique concept, and there is no exception when discussing cyberterrorism.

The best definition of **cyberterrorism** reiterates the aforementioned criteria and refers to "unlawful attacks and threats of attacks against computers, networks and the information stored therein when done to intimidate or coerce a government or its people in furtherance of political or social objectives. Further, to qualify as cyberterrorism, *"an attack should result in violence against persons or property, or at least cause enough harm to generate fear"* (Denning, 2000). The emphasis here is the violence, because at a minimum, without violence an event is not terrorism.

It is understood that cybersecurity is a necessary evil to protect the multitudes of data that exist as part of the digital information age. It is also understood that data is constantly under threat from intruders who seek to access, exploit, damage, or destroy the data, but these acts alone are not terrorism. When data is vandalized, stolen, corrupted, or otherwise used in a nefarious way, this may be the result of intentional malfeasance or criminals. If cybersecurity fails, these attacks are disruptions to our normal process, possibly a nuisance or inconvenience, at worst a crime. These attacks range from silly to serious and costly, but there are almost no cases where a cyberattack resulted in extraordinary violence.

There *could* be examples of cyberattacks resulting in death or serious injury, if, for example, a plane was crashed, or a gas line exploded, or a city traffic system caused accidents—but these types of results *have not occurred*. There are several reasons cyberterrorism is not a reality, but none of them preclude the possibility of cyberterrorism in the future.

The first line of defense against cyberterrorism can be attributed to the organic and wild-west like attributes of the Web. There is no centralized location where all of our information is housed; rather, the Web is an astounding array of interconnected systems, many of them autonomous. If a cyberattack were to occur on one set of data, rendering it useless, it is highly unlikely it would directly affect data stored on a separate unique system. For example, if Facebook were to be attacked and could no longer provide access to your information, this would not have a cascading effect on your local hospital's surgery schedule. Likewise, if a city's sewer treatment plant were to be rendered useless due to a cyberattack, this would not prevent the 911 call center from being able to dispatch resources. Each of these separate and autonomous systems, many built on different software platforms, is physically and technologically isolated. The nature of the Web and its unmonitored growth is ironically one of our best defenses against a cyberthreat.

To further protect many critical infrastructure resources (like power plants, water treatment facilities, air control towers, etc), the systems used are isolated, running on *intranets* with no connection to the Web at all. This is a physical security protocol that creates an "air gap" between the system and the Internet. In order to breach this air gap, a cyberattack would have to be custom built to attack a specialized system that can only be accessed from within. If a successful attack of this nature were undertaken, it is important to understand it would still be an isolated incident—a cyberattack on a water treatment facility in New Orleans would not affect a water treatment facility in Los Angeles.

Attacking the Iranian Nuclear Program

In the summer of 2010, researchers and journalists discovered the existence of a complex computer worm that was spreading through Iran. Called "Stuxnet," a name based on keywords found in the code, the malware was designed to attack specific types of SCADA (supervisory control and data acquisition) systems manufactured by Siemens.

Before we continue discussing Stuxnet, you need to understand a little bit (a very little bit) about SCADA. SCADA systems act as the interface between computers and physical machines and systems. They are used to control power plants, assembly and manufacturing facilities, water treatment plants, transportation systems, research labs, and more. They are typically not very secure simply because they are not supposed to be directly connected to the Internet and therefore cannot be attacked remotely (from a basement in Queens, for example). To exploit (which is IT speak for break in and use without authorization) a SCADA interface, the attacker is assumed to be in physical proximity (inside the room or facility) of the system; once an attacker is inside your physical security (locks and guards), then he or she generally have free reign with data systems. Not to mention that they have free reign with most everything else of value in the organization. Because SCADA systems are not very secure, they form the backbone of every doomsday "cyberterrorism" scenario ever written. Imagine attackers able to use a web browser to reroute trains, overload nuclear power plants, and cause massive blackouts. Keep imagining—it's not going to happen. Remember, administrators know the SCADA vulnerabilities, and because of that SCADA isn't connected to the Internet for a teenager in Queens to break into.

Okay, back to Stuxnet . . .

Computer security analysts reviewed the Stuxnet code in detail and found several attributes to be different from other malware programs. First, it was highly complex and professional code, which is a far cry from the majority of worms and trojans circulating on the Internet. Second, it was very, very specific in which systems it would infect, and if installed on a system that didn't match its target profile, it would lie dormant, causing no issues or disruptions.

Using various exploits to infect Windows computers, the worm was only seeking the specific type of SCADA control interface used by the Iranian government in its nuclear research laboratories. In other words, the worm was targeting the Iranian nuclear program. Once it found the specific Siemens SCADA system and infected it, the worm disrupted the performance of the machines controlled by the system but reported to controllers and administrators that everything was running normally.

In 2010, Iran was moving forward with its nuclear program and was trying to create highly enriched uranium (HEU). Creating HEU is a complex and physical process involving centrifuges that must operate within very tight limits. Throughout 2009, the Natanz nuclear facility in Iran suffered several centrifuge shutdowns and other reductions in HEU production. It is speculated that Stuxnet caused the disruptions and may have damaged or destroyed up to 20% of the facilities centrifuges.

In a 2012 book titled *Confront and Conceal: Obama's Secret Wars and Surprising Use of American Power,* author David Sanger claims that Stuxnet was developed by the National Security Agency in cooperation with Israeli experts specifically to attack Iranian HEU production systems. Researchers in 2013 discovered an early version of the worm, which apparently dates from before 2006, and Sanger's book indicates that development began under President Bush and continued under President Obama. The evidence points to a coordinated and well-orchestrated cyberattack on Iran's nuclear research facilities.

Since 2010, security professionals have shown how Stuxnet could be modified to attack other systems, and the source code can now be downloaded from the Internet. Stuxnet may have the first major cyberattack to have physical consequences, but it certainly won't be the last.

Distributed Denial of Service (DDOS)

This is the most common of the big cyberattacks and occurs when multiple systems are inflected with a trojan used to attack a single system. By hitting one Internet-based system from multiple sources, it makes the attack almost impossible to block, and attacking system can be difficult to differentiate from legitimate users.

In March 2013 one of the largest DDOS attacks (300 GBps) occurred primarily on systems in Europe and was thought to have significantly slowed the flow of data being transmitted. However, despite this attack, at no point did the Internet "break" and at no point were lives in danger.

There have been cyberattacks in the past that have coincided with political movements or been perpetrated by terror groups, but none of them can be considered terror attacks because of their obvious lack of violence. Examples include:

- In 1998 the Tamil Tigers of Sri Lanka bombarded Sri Lankan embassies with emails, totaling over 800 a day, over a two-week period intended to disrupt communications.
- In 2000 the Japanese government discovered the software system they used to track police vehicles had been developed by the religious dissident group Aum Shinryko who were responsible for the 1995 Sarin gas attacks on the Tokyo subway system.
- In 2010 the "hacktavist" group WikiLeaks published 76,900 documents on the U.S. conflict in Afghanistan, and 400,000 documents related to the war in Iraq. Many of the documents leaked were classified and included diplomatic cables.
- In 2013 the cybergroup Anonymous claimed responsibility for hacking the U.S. Sentencing Commissions website as part of "Operation Last Resort".

While cyber crime and possible DDOS events are a reality, the future where cyberattack events result in actual violence or deaths has yet to be realized. While our lives are ever more interdependent on the technology around us, it is also assumed that cybersecurity measures will continue to be aggressively pursued.

Piracy

Piracy is an old profession, and as soon as man began putting vessels in the seas pirates soon followed. Homer's poems, the *Iliad* and the *Odyssey*, written around 800 B.C.E. and considered the oldest examples of Western literature, refer to sea bandits and maritime raids. Like criminals, **pirates** are nothing more than thieves on the water, raiding and plundering other people's ships.

Organized maritime piracy has been on the rise in the past decade; specifically, piracy off the Horn of Africa has contributed to this increase. Large-scale attacks off the coast of Somalia in 2006–2008 drew international attention and resulted in increased participation in the multinational coalition task force.

International Interdictions

Combined Task Force 150 was a U.S. Navy formation that was repurposed after September 11, 2001, to patrol the waters off the Horn of Africa. Now a true multinational coalition, ships from the navies of Canada, France, Japan, Denmark, Germany, and the United Kingdom contribute to its mission of maritime safety. Since 2006 CTF-150 has been specifically engaged in anti-piracy efforts off the coast of Somalia and has conducted joint operations with Chinese, Russian, and Indian navies. CTF-150 has also been engaged in interdiction and maritime cordons in the Indian Ocean to prevent the escape of al Qaeda members from Somalia.

As a criminal enterprise, piracy rarely is conducted with the intention of intimidating or influencing a population or government. In a review of the definitions of terrorism, all include the concept of change or provocation as a key component, despite the lack of a single universal definition. In 2004 the UN Security Council came close to an agreed upon definition in its "Resolution Strongly Condemning Terrorism" and emphasized that terrorism has as its purpose, " . . . to provoke a state of terror in the general public or in a group of persons or particular persons, intimidate a population or compel a government or an international organization to do or to abstain from doing any act . . . ". While contemporary pirates could provoke a state of terror and have created the need for international maritime security forces, they do not have a political agenda, and they are exclusively profit oriented. Without a unifying purpose, the category of piracy can only be considered a means to an end and not part of the terrorism spectrum.

The United Nations and Maritime Safety

In 2005 the UN adopted the "Convention for the Suppression of Unlawful Acts Against the Safety of Maritime Navigation," which references the 1994 UN General Assembly Declaration on Measures to Eliminate International Terrorism. The 2005 Safety of Maritime Navigation does not redefine maritime crimes in terms of terrorism; rather, it adds references to other appropriate legislation. The additional text provided by the UN sought to bolster overall maritime security understandings and asked states to consider taking individual appropriate measures through legislation. It is important to note that nowhere did the UN's maritime resolution imply piracy was the same as terrorism.

Key Terms

Criminal terrorism	Military dissident terrorism
Guerillas	Narcoterrorism
Paramilitary	FARC
Militias	Cyberterrorism
Dark networks	Pirates
Bright networks	

Discussion Questions

1. What is an example of a bright terror network?

2. What could be an example of cyberterrorism?

3. Why does the presence of a uniform change how we define terrorists?

References

Chaliand, B. (2007). *The history of terrorism from antiquity to al Qaeda.* Berkeley: University of California Press.

Sanger, D. E. (2012). *Confront and conceal: Obama's secret wars and surprising use of American power.* New York: Crown Publishers.

Terrorist Threats to the United States, Testimony Before the House (House Special Oversight Panel on Terrorism, May 23, 2000).

United Nations General Assembly GA/L/3433. (2012, October 8). Legal Committee Urges Conclusion of Draft Comprehensive Convention on International Terrorism. *Sixty-seventh General Assembly, Sixth Committee, 1st & 2nd Meetings.* New York: UN Department of Public Information.

Chapter 7

Terrorism Models

I t is a straightforward observation to state, "not all terrorist organizations are the same." They vary in purpose, size, organizational methods, tactics, and geography. Even two organizations with similar declared purposes in close proximity to one another may have vastly different organizational structures. To complicate our understanding of terrorist organizational models, we have seen far-reaching changes in how some terrorist organizations work and what risks they are willing to accept. Modern religious terrorists such as al Qaeda operate with a different set of rules than terrorist organizations from the 1960s or 1970s.

This chapter will explore the different organizational models used by terrorist organizations, as well as evolution in these models we have seen over the past decades. Recognizing and understanding the different ways terrorist organizations work is important because this determines how we respond to and mitigate the threats.

Terrorist Organizational Structures

Terrorist organizations have . . . organization. They have a structure, people, and other resources to help them stay on track and accomplish their objectives. There are a variety of structures that can be adopted or adapted by a group of terrorists, but each of these has one thing in common: the cell. Each network or organization builds upward from the basic cell, and some organizations may not go beyond a single cell organization.

The Terrorist Organization Building Block: The Cell

The most basic terrorist organizational structure, and the one shared by any terrorist organization is the **cell**. Cells are small self-reliant groups within a larger terrorist organization structure. Typically consisting of three to eight people, the cell is the standard tactical element of terrorism—the cell plans and carries out the attack. Multiple cells may work together, but even in these cases the cells remain separate and distinct.

This separation is what makes cells the preferred structure in the terrorism world. Each cell is self-contained, and communication between cells is limited, with only a single member (typically the cell leader) knowing how to contact other cells. This communications scheme is not efficient, but it is secure. If a cell is arrested or infiltrated by law enforcement or an intelligence agency, there is not a communications trail leading to other cells in the terrorist organization. This prevents a single law enforcement or intelligence breakthrough from compromising other cells or the entire parent organization.

Cell members remain in close contact with one another. They form tight bonds and understand that what little personal safety they might have is provided by the cell itself. Terrorist organizations may consist of one or more cells. In multi-cell organizations, specific cells may be assigned to a geographic region or area, or cells may be given functionally specific tasks or missions. For example, a specific cell may be in charge of target reconnaissance, material acquisition, or other logistical duties.

How cells relate to other cells in the terrorist organization is the basis for defining what type of structure a terrorist organization has adopted. There are two main structures: hierarchal and networked. The terrorist organization may adopt one of these or construct a hybrid of the two.

Hierarchal Organizations

Hierarchal organizations have a visible top-down structure with clearly defined chains of command. There is a clear leader, who in turn commands subordinates, who command their own subordinates. Each member of the organization has a commander or superior who provides direct command and control. In turn, that commander has a superior, and so on and so forth; this chain continues all the way to the top of the organization. In this structure, information and coordination flows vertically (from top to bottom) through the chain of command, but the organization may find it difficult to move information horizontally among cells.

Hierarchal organizations are good at providing centralized identity, mission, and purpose for all of their members since these values flow downward from the overall commander of the organization. Everyone receives the same message.

Cells in a hierarchal organization answer to the cell above them in the structure. Even here, only the cell commander can communicate up or down the

"A hierarchal organization"

chain. It is more likely to see cells with specialized missions in a hierarchical orga-nization. Here, a single logistics cell can assist several other cells with obtaining documents, intelligence, and materials. This type of resource sharing is difficult without a hierarchical command and control structure.

Network Organizations

Networks can take many shapes and sizes. They can exist in the physical world (such as groups of friends, co-workers, business contacts, or terrorists), or they can exist virtually (such as cell phone networks, social media networks, and so on). Each individual entity in the network, whether that is a person or a commu-nications device, is called a **node**. Nodes link together in a variety of patterns, and these links are what enables communication and coordination to occur. Again, these linkages can be physical, such as face-to-face communication between co-workers, or virtual, such as social media posts or email.

Some nodes in a network are more important to the flow of information than others. Let's use a practical example to illustrate this.

Picture your Facebook account (you have one, right)? In your account, you have a list of friends that you know from high school, university, your different jobs, your family, and so on. In each of these groups of friends, it is safe to say that many of your contacts are friends with many of your other contacts—you all "know each other." Your high school friends are grouped together, your col-lege friends are grouped, and seldom do these groups intersect. In effect, all of your Facebook friends form a network organization, and each of your subsets of friends form slightly different networks.

In this hypothetical Facebook model, you are the common link between all these separate subsets of your network, right? Congratulations, you are a **gateway** between these different subsets. If someone in your group of college friends wanted to communicate with someone from your high school subset, that communication would likely go through you; the gateway provides a link between two different networks. The more friends that you have, the more likely you are to act as a gateway.

If your computer stopped working properly and you needed repair advice, or you needed information on how to brine and cook a Thanksgiving turkey, you probably know one or two experts that could help you with your problem. That person may be a friend or a relative, but he or she has some expert knowledge on the topic you need help with; he or she is a **maven**. A maven is an expert, but also more. Mavens can communicate ideas to people who don't already understand them, they can help people see value in a concept or solution, and they are salespeople. If you know someone who will talk to you endlessly about the superiority of the Apple iPhone, and he is factual about it, then you know a maven.

The manner in which nodes in a network are arranged in relation to one another is called the **network topology**.

Chain Networks

Chain networks link nodes in a linear or near linear fashion. Each node will typically have two other nodes connected to it, one on either side. This network topology is useful in logistics operations, where goods and information flows along the network, eventually reaching the desired destination. This topology is also common among smuggling networks—for the same reasons.

Each node in a chain network operates as a gateway node; all traffic passes through each node. This allows for command and control to be exerted through the chain network. All messages can originate from a source (leadership) node and the same message should be, in theory, received across the entire chain network. The limited connections in each node increased security as well. If a single node is compromised, it can lead to only two other nodes, which can in turn lead to others, but this is a time and labor-intensive process.

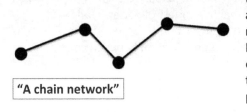

"A chain network"

Hub Networks

Hub networks connect the nodes to a central hub node. This network topology forces all information flow through the central node, which serves as a gateway to the remainder of the network. In some variations, the outer nodes have limited direct connections to other outer nodes, but the primary information conduit remains the hub. The central node has the ability to see and monitor all traffic as it moves around the network. This makes this topology ideal for financial networks or other situations that require oversight or logging.

The hub network often exists in terrorist organizations as a linkage to subnetworks or outside organizations. See the figure below.

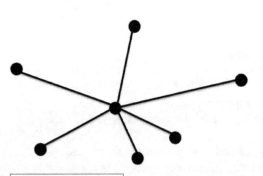

"A hub network"

Mesh or All-Channel Networks

In the **mesh** or **all-channel** network, each node is connected to and may communicate with all other nodes. In effect, every node can talk to any other without any intermediaries and or gateways. This arrangement is efficient for passing information and coordination, but without a central hub or defined starting or end points, there is no central point of influence.

While the mesh network is efficient for communication, it also poses a higher security risk to the terrorist organization. Since each node can communicate with all the others, these linkages can be used to track down the entire network once a single node is compromised by law enforcement or intelligence.

Most operational terrorist networks will be a hybrid of these topologies, depending on the purpose of the subnetworks and the perceived security risks. The hierarchal organization that we discussed first can be modeled as a hybrid of hub, chain, and mesh networks, creating the appearance and functionality of the class is a top-down command structure.

Further, the cell is best modeled as a three- to eight-node mesh network. All cell members (nodes) know and communicate with each other. The cell leader acts as a gateway to a larger hub, chain, or mesh network from which the cell receives instructions and information.

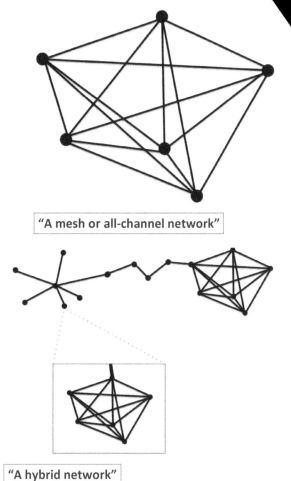

"A mesh or all-channel network"

"A hybrid network"

Single Actor Terrorists: The "Lone Wolf"

Single actor terrorists (or small actor terrorists) conceive, plan, and carry out terrorist attacks without significant support from any known terrorist network or organization. These **lone wolf** terrorists are considered a significant threat due to the fact that without network support and communication, they can be difficult to detect and interdict prior to carrying out their attack.

This threat illustrates the greatest value of terrorist networks to the counter-terrorism analysts—these networks provide a handhold on tracking and understanding terrorist organizations. Since 9/11, the intelligence community and the media have talked about "chatter" as indicators of terrorist plans and activities. This **chatter** is best understood as intercepted terrorist network activity—snippets of overheard conversations, electronic intercepts of phone and email

...tured documents, and **pocket litter** (notes, scraps of paper, and other ... the possession of an enemy combatant when detained or captured). ...aterial gives analysts a fragmentary view of the communication happening inside the network.

With single- or small-actor terrorists, who operate as a single cell without outside communication, counterterrorism analysts and intelligence professionals are denied a valuable tool in identifying terrorists before they can strike.

Ideological Franchising

Without outside network communication, how do single or small actor terrorists develop? Why are most modern terrorist organizations considered to be "al Qaeda affiliates" by the intelligence community and the media?

The answer is **ideological franchising**. Through this process, extremists can adopt the platform of beliefs of a larger terrorist organization and become an affiliate without any direct network connection the larger organization.

Consider Subway Sandwiches. This is a popular sandwich franchise, with over 38,000 stores in operation in over 100 countries (Doctors Associates, 2013). These stores pay a fee for the use of the Subway name, logo, recipes, and other branding material, but they are not owned by Doctors Associates, the company that owns the subway name. These stores are **franchises** of Doctors Associates; they are independently owned and operated. Why?

Let's say you wanted to open a sandwich shop. You could do all the research, create your own sandwiches, and open "Your Name Sandwiches," or you could pay the fee to Doctors Associates and open a Subway, complete with known recipes, menus, and branding. Why would you want to franchise? Name recognition. Your potential customers already know what Subway is, what kinds of sandwiches it sells, and approximately how much they will cost. This isn't to say that Subway is better than Your Name Sandwiches, but it is certainly more recognizable.

The same can (and does) happen with terrorist organizations. A terrorist organization can increase the visibility, and therefore the threat, of its cause by aligning ideologically with a well-known and dangerous terrorist organization such as al Qaeda or the Palestinian Liberation Organization. The immediate capability of the affiliated (or franchised) terrorist organization does not increase, but the **perceived threat** of the newly affiliated organization increases dramatically. Just by embracing a larger name, the affiliate appears to be more dangerous.

Al Qaeda has embraced this model of ideological franchising in the past decade. After 9/11, U.S. military and intelligence operations in Afghanistan and elsewhere put tremendous pressure on the original al Qaeda organization. This pressure reduced or eliminated that ability for the al Qaeda organization to operate, particularly as its networks were systematically identified and compromised. To counter the threat of reduced viability in the world, al Qaeda took to the internet, spreading the message of its platform of beliefs across cyberspace. It did not take long for terrorist and extremist individuals to flock to these beliefs and declare their affiliation with al Qaeda. At this point, the al Qaeda *brand* continued to grow in power and reach, even while the core organizational network was being suppressed to the point of ineffectiveness.

The Boston Marathon Bombing

On the morning of Monday, April 15, 2013, over 23,000 runners began one of the largest road races in the United States. Held on Patriots Day, the Boston Marathon represents one of the largest sporting events in the United States. In fact, after the Super Bowl, the race attracts the second largest number of spectators to an American sporting event.

Shortly before 3:00 PM, with over 5,700 runners still on the course, two improvised explosive devices exploded near the finish line on Boylston Street in Boston. The explosions were located approximately 100 meters apart and detonated within 12 seconds of each other. Media coverage of the race was extensive, and video of the explosions flooded television and internet outlets within minutes. The blasts killed 3 and injured over 250, including dozens of amputations and critical injuries. It was clear immediately that this was a terrorist event, but how did this happen? The grandstand and finish line areas were swept for explosives twice that day, with the latest sweep occurring an hour before the attack. There was a massive law enforcement presence around the finish line (and throughout the city), but the area was a picture perfect example of a soft target.

Access to the finish line area was not restricted . . . it's a public street in downtown Boston. There were no screenings or bag checks, and that vulnerability is what the attackers exploited. Two brothers, Dzhokhar and Tamerlan Tsarnaev, carried backpacks containing explosive devices into the finish line area, dropped them, and walked away before they detonated. The explosives were homemade, fashioned from pressure cookers filled with shrapnel and black powder probably taken from fireworks.

As the week progressed, authorities utilized surveillance images as well as photos taken by the crowd to identify the two bombers. On Thursday, April 18th, the FBI and Boston Police released images of the brothers in the crowd before the explosions and asked the public for help in identifying the attackers. Eyewitness reports corroborated the video evidence—the FBI was certain these two men were involved.

Within hours of their photos being circulated on every media outlet in the nation, the Tsarnaev brothers went on the offensive. They shot and killed an MIT police officer,

(Continued)

and then carjacked a vehicle and kidnapped the driver. Their actions that week showed they had not planned an escape from the city and were not prepared for the events that followed. In short, they were amateurs. After the carjacking victim escaped (amateurs, remember), police closed in and engaged the suspects in a firefight. The older brother, Tamerlan, was killed in the exchange of fire, and Dzhokhar fled. One of the largest manhunts in the United States effectively shut down Watertown, a suburb of Boston, as police went door to door in search of the terrorist. Dzhokhar was located hiding, wounded, in a boat in the backyard of a house in Watertown. After a brief confrontation with police, he was captured . . . ending one of the most dramatic weeks in recent American memory.

As he was questioned, Dzhokhar revealed that his older brother Tamerlan was the mastermind of the plot, and the attacks were in response to the killing of Muslims in Iraq and Afghanistan. The Tsarnaev family emigrated legally from the Chechnya region of Russia and were Muslim; reports indicate Tamerlan had become increasingly devout in the three years prior to the attack. The Russian security services had requested the FBI question Tamerlan, labeling him as a possible extremist. The FBI interviewed the older Tsarnaev in 2011, but did not find any links to terrorism or extremist activity. Tamerlan spent six months in Russia in 2012, but full details of his associations there are not available.

This attack is a perfect example of a lone wolf attack. The Tsarnaev brothers, despite warnings from the Russians, were not on the radar of American authorities. They conceived, planned and executed a devastating attack with no support from an established terrorist organization. Without links to a known terrorist cell, they operated out of sight of authorities, and the first indication they were active was when their devices detonated. This is the worst-case scenario for law enforcement and intelligence officials and represents the greatest terrorist threat to free societies. Despite their Chechen links, the Tsarnaev brothers had been in the United States for a decade, had attended school, and from all indications had radicalized in the United States. Dzhokhar was a naturalized U.S. citizen and was enrolled in a local university. The Boston attack is a good example of both lone wolf behavior as well as domestic radicalization.

This type of ideological franchising will continue to occur as the world becomes increasingly digital and connected. Cyberterrorism may not be possible in our current world, but that does not mean that cyberspace is not a tool for radicalization and terrorism. Nidal Hasan communicated via email with radical clerics in Yemen prior to his attack on Fort Hood, Texas. Other American citizens have been in contact through the Internet with overseas radicals, leading them to increasing extremism and eventual terrorist attacks.

Fort Hood Shooting

On November 5, 2009, Major Nidal Hasan walked into the Soldier Readiness Processing Center on Fort Hood, Texas, and opened fire on uniformed soldiers. Armed with an FN Five-seven pistol and hundreds of rounds of 5.7 mm ammunition, Hasan killed 13 people and wounded 30 more. While most of the casualties were U.S. Army soldiers, they were all unarmed and working to process paperwork for their upcoming deployment to Afghanistan. The shooting rampage ended outside the Processing Center by a Fort Hood police officer who shot Hasan four times.

The Federal Bureau of Investigation determined that Hasan had acted alone, without material or financial support from any domestic or foreign source. Hasan purchased his handgun, extra magazines, and ammunition from a Killeen, Texas, gun store in July 2009. He practiced at public shooting ranges for months before launching his attack. The event is currently classified as "workplace violence," but several analysts and lawmakers have labeled the attack domestic terrorism. Neither the FBI nor the Department of Defense have released any motive for the attacks.

Hasan was born in Virginia to parents who had immigrated to the United States from the West Bank. He was a practicing Muslim, who reportedly grew more devout after the deaths of his parents. He attended university at Virginia Tech and subsequently earned a position in the Uniformed Services University of the Health Sciences, where he earned his medical degree in psychiatry in 2003. He served his internship at Walter Reed Army Medical Center, where supervisors and co-workers expressed concern about his Islamic views, detached attitude, and apparent opposition to the U.S. operations in Afghanistan and Iraq.

Prior to opening fire, Hasan shouted "Allah Akbar!" This statement combined with his Muslim background and stated worldview was enough for some analysts to label this attack as terrorism. To further this argument, the FBI revealed that Hasan had exchanged emails with radical Islamic cleric Anwar al-Awlaki during a period from December 2008 through the summer of 2009. After the attack, al-Awlaki praised Hasan for striking out at America, but would not admit to prompting or encouraging the actual attack.

The emails were investigated at the time by the FBI and the Department of Defense, but were determined to have no indicators of terrorist behavior. Hasan was an active Army psychiatrist, and it was assumed that the messages were research into conflicts Muslim soldiers might have with serving in the U.S. Army. The investigation was dropped.

Without a declared motive, it is difficult to determine if this shooting was terrorism or simply the act of a mentally unstable person. Hasan was scheduled to deploy to Afghanistan three weeks after the shooting and had expressed displeasure with that circumstance. His unhappiness with the Army and history of behavior led the Department of Defense to classify this attack as workplace violence, not terrorism. Hasan's court martial proceedings are still ongoing.

Case Study: Timothy McVeigh and Terry Nichols

Prior to 9/11, the bombing of the Murrah Federal Building in Oklahoma City stood as the most devastating terrorist attack on U.S. soil. On April 19, 1995, a Ryder rental truck carrying over 4,000 pounds of ammonium nitrate/fuel oil (ANFO) exploded in front of the Murrah Federal Building. The attack killed 168 people, including 19 children. The attack was conceived, planned, and carried out by Timothy McVeigh and his co-conspirator, Terry Nichols.

McVeigh was 26 years old at the time of the bombing and had served in the U.S. Army in the Persian Gulf War. He met Nichols first while they both were in the Army, although Nichols' enlistment lasted only a year. After McVeigh left the Army at the end of 1991, he built a simple and nomadic life. He was vocal of his criticisms of the U.S. government, and in later interviews stated that he began fostering anti-government feelings during his service in the Gulf War.

In 1993, McVeigh drove to Waco, Texas, to show his support for the Branch Davidians under siege by the FBI and Bureau of Alcohol, Tobacco, and Firearms. He was photographed selling pro-gun bumper stickers from the hood of his car, and by this time was vocally anti-government.

Around this time, he renewed his association with Nichols and began producing anti-government literature and videos. Some reports indicate that Nichols and McVeigh were experimenting with the construction of explosive devices, building upon the experience McVeigh gained while serving in the Army. McVeigh discussed several options for attacking the U.S. government, believing it guilty of betraying the Constitution of the United States. McVeigh and Nichols ultimately settled on a tactic—bombing—and a target—the Murrah Building. Several other actions were considered, including assassinations, but the men believed a bombing was the most effective way to carry out an attack.

After the bombing, McVeigh and Nichols were arrested, tried, and ultimately found guilty of using a weapon of mass destruction, murder, and attempted murder. While in prison, McVeigh granted very few interviews, but ultimately declared his motives for the attack were simple—revenge against the government for years of violence, betrayal, and injustice. McVeigh never admitted to knowing there were children in the Murrah Building, but since the daycare was visible from the street, it seems impossible that he was ignorant of their presence. Nichols was sentenced to life in prison without any possibility of parole. McVeigh was executed by lethal injection in 2001.

Terrorist Organization Evolution: From "Old" to "New"

Many Americans equate terrorism with the horrific events of September 11, 2001. The horrific attacks of that day, and the ongoing "War on Terrorism," have put a distinctive face on terrorism that is very different from what societies around the world had been struggling with for decades (and longer). In short, the United

States was violently introduced to a "new" brand of terrorism, one that was drastically different from what had come before.

There is no exact date we can point to and say, "terrorism was different after that day"; the evolution is ongoing and gradual. 9/11 has become a focal point for American society, but it was not the moment that "terrorism changed"; it is simply the moment where most of us realized it. We can look at the evolution and categorize it into four main areas: organization size and structure, ideology, constituents, and methods.

Organization Size and Structure

Terrorist organizations are getting smaller. As we have shown earlier in this chapter, terrorist networks are a foothold for counterterrorism efforts to gain traction. The larger the network, the easier it is to identify and compromise. Terrorists are rational, intelligent people, and they realize this. As intelligence and law enforcement agencies become more adept at using network size and structure against terrorist groups, they simply get smaller. The cell becomes more independent, perhaps even completely cut off from the main terrorist network. Only the most general of instructions and goals are given to the cell before communications are severed.

Terrorist organization in the "old" model may have boasted hundreds, if not thousands of active members and supporters. Current groups, who operate in the "new" model are considerably smaller—dozens of members, or fewer. They maintain their ideological ties (their franchise) by using technology and the Internet. But without the formal links and networks of the old model, they are difficult to identify and track.

This reduction in size eliminates the traditional hierarchal command and control structures as well as centralized direction and mission tasking. The smaller, agile, cell-based networks take general guidance from nominal leaders and build their own missions and objectives. This distributed style is again difficult to track, but it can result in a fractured ideology or geopolitical platform. Without centralized control and guidance, individual cells may decide on different operational priorities or methodology. The tradeoff here is improved security and agility versus a consistent, unified message and method. This trend is a direct result of ideological franchising.

Smaller groups provide additional security for the terrorists in other ways. Old-model terrorist organizations, with hundreds of members, were open to infiltration by law enforcement or government agents. It was impossible for everyone in the organization to personally know everyone else. With smaller terrorist organizations in the new model, the cells often draw from single families, clans, or tribes. It is impossible to infiltrate a terrorist organization where everyone is related by marriage and blood to everyone else. Impossible. This lack of variety in the backgrounds of the members creates heterogeneous belief structures—everyone has the same background and similar if not identical belief systems. This leads to a nearly automatic cohesiveness in belief that old model terrorists had to work years to obtain. Finally, this cohesive belief system allows the smaller group to resist fracturing and splintering like many larger terrorist organizations have done in the past.

Ideology

We discuss what drives different types of terrorists in other parts of this text, but it is significant to look at the shifts in how ideology motivates terrorism overall. **Ideology** is defined as a system of concepts or ideas and a manner of thinking that is common to an individual or group. It is important to understand that ideology is a call to action, not simply a static belief system. Ideology moves people to do something, to belong to something, and to defend something.

In the 1970s and 1980s, the foremost terrorist organizations were based on dissident concepts and geopolitical motivations. Their ideology was based on the political, ethnic, or nationalistic goals and ideology; they were focused on a place and time. Even groups involved in conflicts influenced by religion, such as the numerous Palestinian terrorist groups, were primarily geopolitically motivated. Religion was secondary.

In our modern era, the new-model terrorists are predominately religiously motivated. Islamic Jihad and al Qaeda are not fighting for nationalist values or political gain, they are waging war against Western values and institutions based on the perceived commands of God. This religious guidance and motivation is new, and it creates a dangerous and violent terrorist. Further, these new religious terrorists do not think they can fail, since they are following divine guidance in waging jihad.

This shift from a dissident model to religious model has created an expanded, apocalyptic model of terrorism, which we will discuss momentarily.

Constituents

Old-model terrorists, who we just established were primarily dissident terrorists, viewed themselves as fighting for someone. They were acting on behalf of an oppressed ethnic or national group; they had **constituents**. In much the same way that elected representatives are expected to represent their people while working in government, these dissident terrorist groups were representing populations who had no other way to express their frustration.

Politicians take actions to appease their constituent populations, even actions that might go against what they personally want to do. This is required to maintain the support of the constituent population, without which the politician would quickly find himself or herself out of a job. In a similar manner, old-model terrorist organizations had to fit their actions and attacks to the desires of their constituent populations. If they failed to do so, support for the cause in those populations would shift or dry up, leaving the terrorist organization in a precarious and dangerous position. In many ways, having a constituent base acts as a limiter on the type and scope of attacks the terrorist organization will carry out. It is one thing to support a terrorist organization that is striking out at the government or the military, but it is another level of support to condone attacks that kill hundreds of bystanders.

New-model terrorists do not directly serve a constituent population, and this has significant impacts on how those organizations operate. Without the limiting factors required by the need to maintain the support of a population, terrorists are free to plan and execute larger and more violent attacks. In many ways, the new model ideology casts off the need of constituents and creates a terrorist organization acting only to satisfy the leadership of the organization. We've moved from requiring approval and support of thousands of people to requiring the support of a handful of violent extremists. When you combine that with the homogenous nature of the cultural and belief systems in that tiny cadre, it is a recipe for bigger and more devastating attacks, without limits on targets or casualties.

Methods

Terrorists are moving away from small, sure attacks toward high-profile attacks with greater risk of failure. Instead of small bombings of government buildings, new-model terrorists prefer large, terrifying events against public transportation or other civilian interests. Hijackings have given way to the 9/11 attacks. Kidnappings have been replaced with WMD threats.

The new-model terrorist, without a need of constituent approval, is free to use indiscriminate devastation on a scale that would be unthinkable to a dissident terrorist of the 1960s or 1970s. An attack in 1975 might kill a dozen people. The 1995 Aum Shrinko Sarin attack killed 12, but was intended to kill many more. The August 1998 Embassy bombings in Tanzania and Kenya killed 223. The 9/11 attacks killed almost 3,000.

In 1988, terrorism analyst Brian Jenkins wrote, "terrorists want a lot of people watching and a lot of people listening and not a lot of people dead." This statement reflected the fact that terrorists used their attacks and activities to engage an audience with a specific message. In 2006, Jenkins revisited his own passage and concluded that terrorists are losing some of their restraint, and attacks are becoming bloodier (Jenkins, 2006).

Counterterrorism and intelligence experts have long been concerned about terrorist organizations acquiring and using a weapon of mass destruction. These scenarios involving chemical, biological, or nuclear weapons could potentially kill thousands of people just about anywhere in the world. Old-model terrorists, concerned about public support and self-image, would not utilize these types of weapons. Only the new terrorists, driven by religious fervor and certitude would think of employing weapons that would kill or maim thousands; only a group with such apocalyptic views would fail to consider the backlash that such an attack would generate.

Is Terrorism Actually Evolving?

We have discussed the evolution of terrorism . . . but is it evolving, or is the dominant form of terrorism simply changed in the past fifteen years? In other words, if a "traditional" terrorist organization in the vein of the IRA or PLO became active again, would it operate under the model of "new terrorism" or rely on the tactics that served those organizations in decades past?

The reality is that dissident terrorist organizations must operate with their constituent populations in mind. Violence remains a tool for attention, and excessive violence may remain counterproductive as it can reduce support and sympathy.

This progression from old to new is valuable to analysts as we try to understand our enemy. It is not, however, useful in trying to predict how terrorism will be shaped in the future. The evolution of terrorism relates directly to the types of terrorism active worldwide as well as access to new technologies and weapons. Will religious terrorism continue to dominate the field for the next 50 years? Maybe not. Will we see the rise of a new dominant type of terrorism? Possibly. When that happens, it is safe to say that terrorism as a whole will evolve again. To date, with the exception of the Aum Shrinko attacks in the mid-1990s, no terrorist organization has used, or even attempted to use, a WMD. This is despite nearly 20 years of planning and preparing for such an attack. Predicting the general terrorist trends and behavior is a difficult endeavor.

Key Terms

Cell	Ideology
Chain network	Lone wolf
Chatter	Maven
Constituents	Mesh or all-channel network
Franchises	Network topology
Gateway	Node
Hierarchal organizations	Perceived threat
Hub network	Pocket litter (Kaleem, 2013)
Ideological franchising	Single-actor terrorist

Discussion Questions

1. How does an open society such as the United States counter the threat of homegrown, lone-wolf terrorists?

2. How will terrorism evolve in the future? Will methods continue to be as ultraviolent as we see today, or will we see a return to more "tame" terrorism?

3. Are new-era religious terrorists ignoring their constituents, or are their constituents demanding an increasing scale of violence?

References

Jenkins, B. M. (2006). *The New Age of Terrorism. The McGraw-Hill Homeland Security Handbook.* Retrieved from www.rand.org/pubs/reprints/RP1215.

Kaleem, J. (2013, April 19). Boston bombing suspects' Muslim identity provides few clues to motivation for bombing. Retrieved May 2, 2013, from Huffington Post: www.huffingtonpost.com/2013/04/19/boston-bombing-suspects-muslim_n_3116299.html

Schmitt, E., Schmidt, M. S., & Barry, E. (2013, April 20). *Inquiry Shifts to Suspect's Russian Trip.* Retrieved May 2, 2013, from The New York Times: www.nytimes.com/2013/04/21/us/boston-marathon-bombings.html?_r=0

Tangel, A., & Powers, A. (2013, April 20). FBI: Boston suspect Tamerlan Tsarnaev followed 'radical Islam'. Retrieved May 2, 2013, from Los Angeles Times: http://articles.latimes.com/2013/apr/20/nation/la-na-nn-boston-bombing-suspect-radical-fbi-20130420

Chapter 8

The Media and Terrorism

Ask yourself, if there was no media coverage would we still have terrorism? In order for terrorism to be effective, it has to draw attention to a cause, and the media fills this role. This creates a symbolic relationship between the media and the terror group, an interdependence and mutual need, and the media is sometimes called "The Handmaiden to Terrorists." Terrorism is political theatre and the media needs news to fulfill its mission; the terror group needs the media to spread its mission, as a team they give context to an event.

Terrorism includes acts of extraordinary violence, or possibly the threat of great violence, and the media is the messenger of these events. It goes without saying that no reporter or editor wishes for terrorism or mass death. It is important to remember the media are messengers of many events, not just terrorism, and conceptually the media is the link between events and communities.

It is interesting to look at **punctuated events** in history, which are moments of profound significance. In a punctuated event, like 9/11 in the United States, there are profound shifts in perception and understanding after the event takes place. The media facilitates and shapes our reactions and allows us to measure what is occurring.

The role of the media is changing, in part because of new technologies but also because of shifts in culture regarding information. The information that is flowing from the media, through peer-to-peer, and portable communication devices allows us data access at a rate that is growing greater than exponentially. The amount of information generated between the birth of the world and 2003 was estimated at 5 exabytes. Most of you are asking, "What's an exabyte?" The answer is 10^{18} bytes; it's a lot. In 2011 we were generating the same amount of information, 5 exabytes, every two days. Think about that for a minute. We create the same amount of information every two days that we spent the first 6,000 years of recorded history creating.

Interestingly, this growth in access to information has changed the way terrorists, extremists, and people with a political agenda can reach the public. It is no longer just the media who informs you, but the consumer who informs the media. Think about the last viral video or interesting tidbit of information a friend sent you, and the fact it became reportable news *after you had already seen it*. CNN or Fox ran the "story" at least a day after you had already consumed that information. Information and the ability to share it has unlimited potential. The media has an additional burden because you, the consumer, ultimately evaluate its effectiveness.

Semantics and Negativity

Semantics includes the words we choose to describe people and situations. There are options in how the media can portray events or people, and this choice of words is part of what conveys **media bias.** It is part of marketing that specific media outlets portray the information and news with a given bias. If you are asked to name a conservative media news channel, you could easily do it. The same is true for a liberal media outlet, or particular types of publications. The presence of media bias is not a problem as long as the audience is aware of the bias.

We humans are fascinated by bad news and react more powerfully to negative information than neutral or positive information. Ironically, we believe negative information has more actual information and is more important than positive data. We are also more influenced by negative outcomes than we are actual outcomes. For example, if a doctor says you have a 50% chance of dying, we find this much more informative than if a doctor tells of we have a 50% chance of survival. This obsession with bad news is called a **negativity bias,** and the media is well aware that we prefer drama when we search for information. The influence of the negativity bias is incredibly important because it means we focus not on what is happening but what *could* happen. The negative emotions we associate with a possible terror attack can overwhelm the reality or the probability of the threat.

Negativity Bias and the One Percent Doctrine

When you conduct a **threat assessment** you measure two components: **probability** and **impact**. The *probability* is the likelihood that an event will occur, and the *impact* is the result if the event did occur. For example, if you live in California, a high-probability, high-impact event would be an earthquake. Because earthquakes have occurred before, and they will probably occur again, you have high probability. Earthquakes in California have historically done extensive damage, so it is fair to estimate future events will also have high impact. Given the high-probability, high-impact estimation, it is reasonable to allocate resources (time, energy, money) to reducing the probability and reducing the impact, if you can.

After 9/11 we began to re-examine threat assessments because flying planes into large buildings had once been considered a low-probability scenario. In an effort to prevent a low probability, high impact events from occurring again Vice President Cheney proposed the "**One Percent Doctrine**" (sometimes called the Cheney Doctrine). The One Percent Doctrine proposed that even if an attack had a 1% chance of happening, we must plan and prepare for it as if it were a certainty. The One Percent Doctrine pushed resources (time, energy, money) for planning and preparing for weapons of mass destruction (WMD) attacks. The problem is that with limited resources, and low-probability events, you can lose sight of high-probability events. The focus on WMDs following 9/11 made high-probability events, like a hurricane in the Gulf of Mexico, less of a priority. In 2005, after Hurricane Katrina, it was clear that prioritizing low-probability events was potentially more deadly than planning for high-probability ones.

The reason threat assessments are used is because they take into account all types of information, including historical events, intelligence gathering, hazard identification, and vulnerabilities. Threat assessments are used to allocate resources in ways they will be most effective, but it is an unfortunate truth that not all threats can be anticipated. Resource allocation must be done wisely, and with knowledge of our negativity bias and obsession with bad news. The One Percent Doctrine works with unlimited resources, but it also means we would have to plan as thoroughly for an alien invasion as we do for storms.

Personal Spin

Obviously, the way we consume news and information has changed dramatically, and the era of a newspaper being thrown on the front porch is long gone. The euphemism "print is dead" resounds when we talk about contemporary media, but the truth is, print is just slow. In the time it takes to print something newsworthy, there are new pieces of information and new perspectives already changing the value of the original word. The availability of new information has made us voracious media consumers, and we are no longer satisfied with one source for our information. Ironically, the desire to consume has probably encouraged media bias. The media uses **spin**, which is interpretation of the events and can include opinion and propaganda, to give information a flavor. In an effort to present a new spin on the same information, media outlets cater now to personal priorities (conservative, liberal, entertainment). Interestingly, the public has increased access to the same sources of information the media does, and is often bypassing the media entirely, eliminating their role as facilitator of information. An example of this can be found during the Boston Marathon bombings when people began listening to the Boston Police radio channel, to directly hear what was happening operationally. In the days that followed all the press conferences given by public officials were streamed over the Internet, allowing people to listen to the same information reporters and media outlets were getting.

What the Media Does

When it comes to terrorism there are several types of messages the media can offer:

- Informational: Something has happened
- Warning: You need to be careful
- Instructional: Please do the following
- Facilitative: Presenting differing perspectives
- Supportive: Community adhesion and resilience

Many of these messages will be provided by the response organizations to the media, and the media in turn will package this information for our consumption. There are famous examples of each of these types of risk communication, and you can probably imagine a few from your lifetime.

Informational

During the avian influenza outbreak Dr. Gerberding, then Director of the CDC, famously said, "The best cure for fear is information." The core of informational risk communication is breaking news. Something significant has happened, and the media are (ideally) reporting live and often continuously. This is the moment when everyone rushes to a television or a computer and begins to learn more about what is going on. Informational breaking news captures our attention, but we have short attention spans, so almost immediately the quest for new data kicks in.

Warnings

At the start of an event the information coverage can be limited so incorporated in the breaking news are warning messages. It is natural after comprehending a

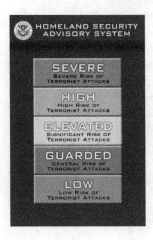

dramatic event to ask, "What is next?" Warning messages are very good media because of our negativity bias. If we are engaged by a negative message, then a warning, which provides the possibility of additional drama and keeps us engaged on the event.

Warning messages that come before an event, or as part of a public information campaign, have had mixed results. Warnings still feed our negativity bias, but sometimes they can backfire because there is confusion over the warning. The classic example of this is the Homeland Security Advisory System (HSAS) that was introduced in 2002 and included five color-coded levels of alertness. Each HSAS level had activities associated with it that both the government and the individual could undertake. The problem with these actions is they were either vague or they were unpublished. For example, at the highest level of alertness,

Red/Severe, citizens were instructed to "be vigilant, and take notice of your sur-roundings." The actions to be triggered by the government at the Red/Severe level included increased law enforcement, but some of these actions were challenged as being unconstitutional. Ultimately, this warning system was deemed a failure and was phased out in 2011.

Instructional

When there is an event, it is a natural human inclination to want to help. We are a participatory culture, obsessed with negativity, and organizations know this. The best example of this can be seen in soliciting donations or support immediately following an event. After disasters, we want to help so much that many people donate blood, even though it is not needed.

The problem with instructional messages is you have to be careful with the messages you distribute (per Voltaire and Stan Lee, *with great power comes great responsibility*). After 9/11 the Department of Homeland Security Director Tom Ridge stated that in the event of a chemical attack citizens should use sheet plastic and duct tape to seal their homes if asked to shelter in place. This immediately created a sense of national urgency and a perception of imminent chemical attacks, so DHS was heavily criticized for being alarmist.

Facilitative

The act of facilitation is to take lots of information and makes it easier to consume. The media is excellent at facilitation, but with a finite amount of facts, often add other information including opinion and interpretation. In order for opinion and interpretation to be considered valid, the media often utilize "**armchair generals**" or experts in the field as commentators. These experts will offer insight into organizational responses and events, but what they provide is spin.

Other types of facilitative media include round table discussion where people of differing opinions discuss or debate and event. These discussions often attempt to understand or predict outcomes of the event and are helpful in providing alternate perspectives. When the media have guests they interview, this also can be seen as a facilitative message. In a sitdown interview, the media will ask a specific individual, often representing an organization or serving as a symbol for a group of people, to provide additional information or insight into an event. These interviews can be revealing in the detail and the emotionality they provide the audience, and they sometimes contribute additional facets of the event.

Supportive

Supportive media coverage is sometimes called **soft news.** This is media coverage of positive or encouraging news and events that offers insight into the recovery process. The best examples of supportive media coverage are when communities are rebuilding, unifying, or coming together. When you see these types of words in a media title, you know it is supportive news. Interestingly, because the media is aware of our negativity bias, supportive news will often be couched in terms of the tragedy rather than the success of the recovery. It is not uncommon for supportive news to open with reiterating the bad news, discussing the optimisms/togetherness/rallying of the community, but then closing with reiterating the tragedy.

Our Expectations

Communication during a major crisis is different than communication in a "normal" day. Major events change the way people react and consume information. People *feel* differently about a major event, and some of the psychological effects on the public can include fear, anxiety, confusion, denial, and a sense of helplessness. Immediately following a major crisis people are concerned about the following questions:

- Are my family and I safe?
- What have you found that may affect me?
- What can I do to protect myself and my family?
- Who caused this?
- Can you fix it?

For answers, people turn to officials and the media as facilitators of those questions. The media has a slightly different perspective and focuses on different questions to include

- What happened?
- Who is in charge?
- Has this been contained?
- Are victims being helped?
- What can we expect?
- What should we do?
- Why did this happen?
- Did you have forewarning?

The gaps between the concerns of the public and the answers the media seeks can create a communication gap that directly affects our perception of the event. One of the worst things the media can do is portray the concerns of the public as irrelevant. This can include the discounting of rumors and myths occurring in real time, or the media appearing paternalistic in their attitude. In order for the media to meet the needs of the public during a crisis, the public must feel empowered, which will reduce the sense of fear and helplessness. The sense of empowerment is achieved through taking action and addressing uncertainty.

We, the consumer, want many different things from the media, often depending upon where in the timeline of the event we are. Regardless of when or how we are getting information it needs to follow the "STARCC Principle":

- **S**imple
- **T**imely
- **A**ccurate
- **R**elevant
- **C**redible
- **C**onsistent

The *simplicity* of the information does not mean the information is dumbed down, it only means that information is provided in small, easily processed bits of information. For example, if you compare these two sentences, it is obvious which one is easier to follow.

Timeliness is getting harder and harder to provide. In the past few terror events much of the information provided at the beginning of the event turned out to be wrong, once verified facts were determined. The consumer is both impatient for information and demanding of facts, which creates timeliness pressure for the media. The media wants to provide you with information, and it wants you to keep using their media product, but the demand for timeliness often occurs at the expense of accuracy

> **Example 1:** *Factions within and political association of various kinds outside parliament took advantage of changing conditions to develop the organizational means of getting their sympathizers elected to office calling their views to public attention. (An excerpt from Turning to Terror by Weinberg in 2011)*
>
> **Example 2:** *The origin of political parties can be found in conditions that allowed people with differing views to be elected to office.*

Accuracy is in a constant fight with timeliness. It takes time to verify information, to make sure it is accurate, and in the rush to provide accuracy *and* timeliness, one of the two is sacrificed. This situation is not uncommon, but the consumer is more and more aware that accuracy is questionable and is using available resources to verify the media's message. This again contributes to an environment where the consumer is the provider of information to the media.

Relevance of information is tricky because in a terrorism event there are complex possibilities regarding who, what, when, where, why, and how (known as the 5Ws and 1 H) of an event. The determination of relevance can be either intelligence or consumer driven, often with armchair generals influencing what is deemed relevant.

Credibility is determined by the person or the origin of the message. When we receive announcements from the Director of the Centers for Disease Control and Prevention (CDC) we believe they are credible because the message is coming from a valid source. We may also believe the credibility of the message based on the actual credentials of the person providing it. For example, the CDC director usually holds a variety of degrees including an MD, giving him or her credentials as a source. The credentialing and credibility can also influence accuracy. For example, when you read domestic policy news from "Jim's Exotic Pets and Check Cashing Blog," the credibility, and accuracy, of the message is tied to the person delivering the information.

Consistency is tied to much of the pervious other points in the STARCC principle and is the cornerstone of reputation. If you have consistently found the information coming from a single source is accurate and relevant, you will return to this source. The consistency of the product is what makes for a repeat customer. Consistency can also be linked to media bias, allowing the opportunity to provide a consistent perspective the user enjoys.

Media and Terrorists

The media has covered terrorism events before, and while the events of 9/11 were often called unprecedented, that is not entirely true. First, the media has been covering large-scale terror attacks for decades, including plane hijackings and bombings. While much of this did not occur inside the United States, there have been other large-scale events that were terrorism. A perfect example is the Oklahoma City Bombing of the Murrah Federal Building in 1995, ensuring adult Americans were familiar with terrorism and buildings as targets. In that same year Japan had the Tokyo Sarin gas attacks on their commuter subway system, perpetrated by a fringe religious group Aum Shinrikyo. Other examples include the Israeli / Palestinian conflict, which had weekly bombings at certain points in its contemporary history. If the conflicts in the Middle East were so commonplace as to be overlooked as benchmark events, the IRA attacks on England in the past 20 years were geographically closer examples we could have learned from.

Also influencing the media is not just the terror event and the end consumer needs, but the source and priority of the media corporation. In most major events of terrorism the coverage provided by domestic media is very different for the coverage by the international media. For example, two weeks after the 9/11 events, a Swiss gunman, Freidrich Leibacher, went on a rampage in a government building and shot 14 people, then himself, in the worst mass killing in Switzerland's history. This act of terrorism in Switzerland, despite occurring so soon after 9/11, was not considered front-page news for U.S. publishers.[1]

There are multitudes of examples where the media determines what information about terrorism is important. Many people do not realize Americans have faced biological attacks before the Amerithrax event. In 1984 a religious cult in Oregon sprinkled *salmonella* (a bacterium that causes diarrhea, fever, and vomiting) on salad bars throughout the town to make the population sick and unable

---

[1]Review of the New York Times and the Wall Street Journal U.S. Edition, for the dates of Sept. 27 & 28, 2001.

to vote in an upcoming election. The cult ultimately sickened 751 people, 45 of whom required hospitalization. This event is considered the largest biological attack in U.S. history, but many people are not even aware it occurred.

The al-Jazeera Phenomenon

Based in the tiny Middle East county of Qatar, al-Jazeera is a 24-hour news channel with unprecedented access and coverage of Middle East events. The influence al-Jazeera has had in promoting news coverage in a part of the world known for censorship cannot be overestimated. Willing to publish any relevant information, al-Jazeera famously broadcast entire Bin Laden videos, often when other media outlets refused. The philosophy behind this type of coverage is *open information media outlet*, which acknowledges media bias, but purposely presents differing biases. This presentation of all perspectives has garnered al-Jazeera some of the most prestigious awards in media coverage, including the Franklin D. Roosevelt Freedom of Speech and Expression Medal and the John F. Kennedy Journalism Grand Prize for International Coverage, both in 2012.

The mentioning of al-Jazeera is not meant to slight the work of other media outlets, but to benchmark open information access models. It is clear from the staggering variety of sources we use to get our information from that consumers are not satisfied with a single source or perspective. However, as reported in 2012 by Kohut et al., there is no clear connection between news formats we use and individual levels of political knowledge. Well-informed people (defined as Americans who were able to correctly answer 15 of 23 political knowledge questions) use a variety of media and an in-depth Pew Research Center survey of over 1,500 adults found that

- 25%–54% use comedy news of either The Daily Show or the Colbert Report
- 26%–54% use major news outlets on the Internet (especially major newspaper websites)
- 19%–54% use broadcast TV
- 27%–54% use National Public Radio Communication Myth vs. Realities

Panic

While it is clear that we are consuming and demanding more information than ever before, there is often a perspective that withholding information is a good idea. There are several communication myths and realities, but one of the most important myths to counteract is the concept of panic. **Panic** is irrational overwhelming fear that causes hysteria and irrationality, and the simple truth of the matter is that *people rarely panic*. In a terror event there are ranges of emotions people will experience, and the most prominent emotion is usually fear. Within fear there can be a range of other emotions including apathy, concern, terror, panic, or denial. But panic, of all the subsets of fear, rarely occurs. If you look at pictures of people immediately after the first World Trade Center was hit by a plane people are running, and moving, but they are not blind with fear, hysterical, or irrational. This means that even during horrible events people can handle the information they are receiving and behave appropriately. The excuse of not sharing information because people will panic is invalid.

Not sharing information can also have the critical fallout of distrust. After the 2011 tsunami hit Japan, one of the nuclear reactors at the Fukushima-Daiichi nuclear power plant began failing. The only way to prevent a nuclear meltdown was to cool the reactor with saltwater, but saltwater would permanently destroy the reactor. Because of the tremendous financial loss associated with destroying the reactor, the company and government representatives delayed the release of information. Eventually, the reactor was pumped with saltwater to prevent a meltdown, but the delay created two realities in the minds of the Japanese people, "First, what might happen next is a potentially bigger problem than what has happened so far; second, governments, experts, and authorities have been consistently behind the curve in talking openly about what might happen next" (Sandman & Lanard, 2011). This reduction in credibility (STARCC Principle) meant that subsequent announcements regarding safety were treated with suspicion.

More Myths

When it comes to terrorism and high-risk events the Federal Emergency Management Agency (FEMA) teaches the myths of communication by Vincent Covello, Director of the Center for Risk Communication in New York City (Lindell, Perry, Prater, & Nicholson, 2006).

" *Myth: Telling the public about a risk is more likely to alarm people than keeping quiet.*
Reality: Information decreases the potential for alarm by giving people a chance to express their concerns. "

While you could argue that you would have felt safer not knowing about the "Amerithrax Attacks" of 2001, imagine how very upset you would be if you found out later —and it had been all kept quiet by the government. Transparency in government is a key to democratic societies, and media is the tool that keeps information flowing. Without information regarding threats and issues the American public would begin to harbor resentment and distrust, known harbingers of political unrest.

" *Myth: We shouldn't go to the public until we have solutions to threats.*
Reality: Release and discuss information about risk management options and involve communities in strategies in which they have a stake. "

Imagine a community receives threats of a biological attack. Someone threatens to poison the local well and, because there is no solution to the threat, leadership decides not to release information about the threat. Obviously, giving people the opportunity to avoid the well water or help solve the problem exponentially increases safety and the possibility of a solution.

This reality was in evidence after the Boston Marathon Bombings of 2013 when the FBI asked the public for their help in sharing any images or video that might shed light on the suspects or the timeline of the attack. By partnering with the community, via the media, law enforcement agencies were able to rapidly identify the culprits.

We can take complicated issues and make them simple. The struggle to understand is often not in the difficulty of the concept, but in the language that is used to describe it. At no point should any communicator underestimate the ability of the general public, who want to know what is going on. During the initial stages of several

66 *Myth: These issues are too difficult for the public to understand.*
Reality: Separate public disagreement with your policies from misunderstanding of technical issues. 99

biological events, complicated medical information was cleanly and clearly communicated to the public. While not terrorism, the H5N1 Avian influenza outbreak, which started in 2006 initially worried people until it was clearly communicated this disease could only be spread to humans through sustained contact with a sick bird. Officials were quick to emphasize the average American does not have sustained contact with wild bird populations who were carrying the virus. Through informed media coverage of this outbreak, which did result in 566 global human infections including 332 deaths, not one American died.

> We are not stupid, nor are we illiterate. As of 2010, in the U.S. population age 18 or greater, over 85% completed high school, and 27% received a bachelor's degree or higher.

In the years following 9/11 and the Amerithrax attacks, organizations with response roles began conducting exercises to prepare and train their communities. The focus of many of these exercises was on biological, chemical, or radiological

66 *Myth: Technical decisions should be left in the hands of technical people.*
Reality: Provide the public with information and involve staff with diverse backgrounds in developing policy. 99

attacks. The purpose of the exercises was to increase awareness and understanding of what an event might bring, but also to identify response problems that could be fixed.

During a particular biological exposure exercise, the decontamination procedures of a hospital were being tested, and one of the people needing decontamination was a law enforcement officer. During decontamination, people who have been exposed are asked to remove all articles of clothing, jewelry, etc. and enter a washing tent where they are scrubbed clean. This created a heretofore unknown complication because the officer was sworn not to relinquish his weapon and had no onsite mechanism to store it properly until the weapon could also be decontaminated. The conflicting needs and directives of various agencies almost brought the exercise to a standstill until a volunteer shouted out, "put the gun in a baggie and he can carry it into the shower." This exemplifies a nontechnical solution to a problem originating in a technicality, with the solution coming from an unexpected source.

❝ *Myth: Risk communication is not my job. Reality: What do you think?* ❞

Albert Schweitzer, winner of the Nobel Peace Prize, famously said, ". . . you don't live in a world all your own. Your brothers are here too." In this age of Web 2.0 and limitless information flow, the truth is we use and evaluate each other as information sources. During terrorist events we look to the individual, on the ground, to provide us with verified information. We use the media as a facilitator, but the search for information includes our fellow man.

Media Case Studies

Whether by design or by accident, the 9/11 events were perfect for media exposure. The targeting of the World Trade Center was astoundingly ambitious, and data showed that on a given workday up to 20,000 people could be in the two buildings. The timing was also impressive, and the gap between after the first plane flew into the World Trade Tower, and the second plane flew into the adjacent tower, ensured the media would be focused on those buildings. These consecutive events, combined with a third plane destroying parts of the Pentagon, allowed the media to speculate on what might be next. Almost immediately large symbolic buildings around the country, like the Sears Tower in Chicago and the CNN building in Atlanta, began evacuations amid concerns they would be next.

We see terrorists again utilizing the media as a utility to spread fear during the 7/7 attacks in London. By targeting a variety of transportation systems, including busses and underground railways, the terrorists brought the entire London transportation system to a halt. By targeting a diversity of locations and types of vehicles, the city was forced to examine every public transportation mode for the possibility of additional bombs.

Terrorist Organizations and the Internet

Everyone uses the Internet, right? Even your parents. Government uses the Internet for outreach and communication, so why would we expect terrorists to ignore the most powerful communications tool ever invented? Well, we don't expect that (right?), and they most certainly utilize the 'net in ways counterterrorism experts wish they wouldn't.

The Internet is about communication, and terrorist organizations utilize it to talk to each other both tactically and strategically, as well as to talk to the public. Email, chat rooms, and message boards provide cheap and easy communications for terrorists. You will note that I don't mention "secure"—that's not an oversight.

Intelligence agencies around the world spend a lot of money on systems to gather electronic communication and track both the content and the parties in the communication. The United States, United Kingdom, Australia, and other partners have allegedly operated a program called ECHELON to intercept digital transmission worldwide for decades (Schmid, 2001). This system can pick out specific messages based on keyword searches, and by this point in the War on Terror has undoubtedly evolved into something even more capable.

Terrorist organizations can use Google too, so the smart ones (the dangerous ones) are aware of these types of capabilities. Why do you think Osama Bin Laden never used a phone or the Internet from his compound in Abbotabad? As a result, sensitive tactical and strategic communication is seldom done over a medium that security services can so easily monitor and track.

Where the Internet shines for terrorists is in outreach. The Internet has changed the way we get information forever. If you wanted to transmit a message to a population in 1970, you needed a TV station, a radio station, or a newspaper. Editors and reporters, not to mention businessmen, controlled those outlets; getting coverage in the media was part and parcel of terrorist motivations. It's why they hijacked planes and carried out attacks. In 2013, if you want to transmit a message to millions of people, all you need is a free Twitter account, or a blog, or file a report on CNN's iReport. The Internet has cut out the middleman and made everyone with a smartphone a broadcaster. This is called *disintermediation*. Audiences can now be directly linked to the creators of information; the media channel middleman has reduced importance.

Terrorists grasp this fact with growing capability. The Internet, including social media, message boards (both open and private), blogs, and traditional websites are used to spread the message of terrorist organizations. Al Qaeda began publishing an online magazine called "Inspire" in late 2010. This magazine is aimed at lone-wolf and self-radicalizing jihadists around the world, and it is printed in excellent American English. It includes how-to articles on bomb making, weapons, and tactics, as well as inspirational stories from successful terrorists and extremists from around the world. It has been widely reported that the Boston Marathon bombers built their explosive devices based on instructions found in the *Inspire* article titled, "How to Make a Bomb in the Kitchen of Your Mom." Catchy.

YouTube and other social media video sites provide a world stage from any terrorist with a video camera or smartphone. Extremists and terrorists use these services as a pulpit from which to preach anti-Western vitriol and hate, and there is little we can do to stop it. Gone are the days when only TV stations and news desks could use a terrorist video message. Now recruitment and operational videos can be published online with ease—all paid for by advertisers.

We link the Internet primarily to religious and Islamic terrorists, but that may simply be because they are the predominant type of terrorist active today. This phenomenon will not diminish; we should expect to see extremists using the latest communications technology from now on.

Interorganizational Dependence

The relationship between the media and terrorists is inextricably intertwined; both need the other for furtherance of their goals. The terrorist organization needs the media to increase exposure to the event and the cause, and the media will respond to this need because their goal is to inform. Without the media terrorism would still exist, and ignoring acts of political violence does not make it go away. The media does have a responsibility to provide information about what is occurring, and ideally this responsibility is carried out in an unbiased way.

The media and terrorist organizations utilize each other, but at no point do they condone or actively support one another. The media, in an effort to discover information they can pass to the consumer, has exposed themselves more and more to dangerous situations. A perfect example of this is Daniel Pearl, an American reporter with dual Israeli citizenship who was working for the *Wall Street Journal*. In 2002 Pearl traveled to Pakistan to explore the link between the attempted terror attack by Richard Reid (the "shoe bomber") and al Qaeda. While in Pakistan, Pearl was kidnapped by a terror group and held for ransom in exchange for all U.S. Pakistani terror detainees, and the continued shipment of F-16 fighter jets to Pakistan. Pearl's kidnappers broadcast his image holding a newspaper with a gun at his head, for the length of his kidnapping. The ransom demands were obviously unmet, and on the ninth day Pearl was beheaded with a sword, and the video was published by the kidnappers.

This infamous event exemplifies the tenuous and dangerous relationship any organization faces in dealing with violent extremists, and the media are no exception.

Key Terms

Punctuated events	Impact
Semantics	One Percent Doctrine
Media bias	Spin
Negativity bias	Armchair generals
Threat assessment	Soft news
Probability	Panic

Discussion Questions

1. What considerations should the media make when reporting an act of terrorism?
2. What is the purpose, and benefit, to media spin?
3. Would a reduction in media coverage influence terror organizations? What about an increase in media coverage?

References

Bongar, B. M., Brown, L. M., Beutler, L. E., Breckenridge, J. N., & Zimbardo, P. G. (2007). *Psychology of terrorism*. New York: Oxford University Press.

Kohut, A., Morin, R., & Keeter, S. (2007). What Americans know: 1989–2007, public knowledge of current affairs little changed by news and information revolutions. *The Pew Research Center for the People & the Press,* 2.

Lindell, M. K., Perry, R. W., Prater, C., & Nicholson, W. C. (2006).Fundamentals of emergency management. FEMA

Sandman, P. M., & Lanard, J. (2003). *Risk communication recommendations for infectious disease outbreaks.* World Health Organization SARS Scientific Research Advisory Committee, Geneva, Switzerland.

Sandman, P. M., & Lanard, J. (2011). It is rational to doubt Fukushima reports. *Nature* 473(7345), 31–31.

Schmid, Gerhard. (2001). *REPORT on the existence of a global system for the interception of private and commercial communications (ECHELON interception system).* Temporary Committee on the ECHELON Interception System, European Parliament. Brussels, Belgium.

Tversky, A., & Kahneman, D. (1986). Rational choice and the framing of decisions. *Journal of Business*, S251–S278.

Chapter 9

Ending Terrorism

We have spent most of this book talking about how terrorism comes to exist, the forms it takes, and the weapons and tactics that terrorists employ. But how do we stop it? The simple answer is this: We can't. We can mitigate the threats or reduce the damage done, but we cannot prevent terrorism from occurring. That is an impossible order.

And yet, we spend billions of dollars every year on security, law enforcement, intelligence operations, and military operations. If we can't stop terrorism, why do we "waste" money trying? The cynical person (or conspiracy theorist) will point to the American military industrial complex and politicians as the driving force behind continued counterterrorism spending. In reality, the simplest answer is the most probable: The government has a duty to protect its citizens. Despite the imperfections of the counterterrorism policy and programs, governments will continue to spend money in the hopes that these programs will have some positive impact on the terrorist threat to citizens.

How Much Money?

The amount of money the United States has spent on counterterrorism since 9/11 is hard to pin down and depends on whether we include the costs of the wars in Afghanistan and Iraq. Estimates from think tanks and government watchdog groups put the amount at between $350 billion and $450 billion domestically, and over $2.5 trillion on foreign combat operations.

The problem is we don't really know what we got for that chunk of money. Granted, there have been no further attacks of the scope and scale of 9/11, but can we definitively link that success to spending?

We are starting to see a reduction in the spending on homeland security and counter terrorism. The Urban Areas Security Initiative (UASI) is a federal grant program designed to enhance metropolitan areas ability to plan, organize, equip, and train for a terrorist attack. In fiscal year 2013, the program had $588 million in available funds; this money is distributed to 25 high-density, high-threat urban areas. That is down from $662 million to 31 urban areas in FY 2011, and $781 million to 60 urban centers in FY 2008 (FEMA, 2013). Congressional review of UASI grants has shown considerable "questionable" spending in recent years. Senator Tom Coburn published a report in 2012 detailing his review of DHS grant spending. In the report, he criticizes the use of federal homeland security money to purchase armored vehicles for small towns and similar equipment purchases. While these types of purchases were once easily justified in the post-9/11 world, fiscal reality is forcing a revised approach to homeland security spending.

Grant funding of equipment and other purchases is only a small aspect of what the United States has done to prevent and "stop" terrorism. All of you have experienced some aspect of counterterrorism policy; some of that may have even been effective. The mandate from the public after 9/11 was that nothing like that could ever be allowed to happen again. That deceptively simple sentiment has driven the foreign and domestic policy of the United States for over 12 years.

Policy and Legislation

In our current counterterrorism era (post-9/11), the United States has created policy and legislation that authorize and govern the War on Terror. These laws and regulations enable the government at multiple levels to investigate, detain, arrest, or attack terrorist organizations and supporters both domestically and abroad.

At the time of this writing, the U.S. Congress was considering or had recently passed 68 bills related to terrorism. Most of this legislation will not ever be voted on by the full Congress or passed into law. Further, many of these bills have only a passing relation to terrorism—the U.S. Congress likes to muddy the waters by combining a variety of topics and provisions into a single bill. For example, bill S. 645 was presented to the Senate and seeks to "reaffirm the United States historic commitment to protecting refugees" (113th Congress, 2013).

Despite the complexity of the U.S. Congress, all federal actions regarding counterterrorism require some form of Congressional approval and oversight. Even existing organizations and programs such as the Department of Homeland Security, the Federal Bureau of Investigation, and the Department of Defense require annual budgetary support from Congress.

Appropriations Bills

It is a foundational concept in the U.S. government that the Congress controls the purse. No other federal entity, including the president of the United States or any Executive Branch department, can appropriate (spend) money. This gives Congress a powerful tool for creating policy: the **appropriations bill**. These bills authorize the government to spend a specific amount of money on specific programs in a specific time frame (typically one year). Since Congress writes these bills, they can, through the allocation and authorization of funds, create priorities in policy and even control the application of existing policy.

Each year, the Congress must pass an annual budget (the primary appropriations bill for the year), which is then signed by the president and becomes law. If Congress and the president are unable to agree on and establish a budget, a **continuing resolution** (or CR) may be passed to fund the federal government temporarily at current spending levels. In addition, Congress may pass supplementary appropriations bills for specialized uses and purposes; these bills are often used for disaster relief and support of military operations. This is not a political science textbook, so we are going to refrain from going into much more detail on this. From a terrorism and counterterrorism perspective, it is important to understand these concepts because appropriations bills are where the federal government sets a great deal of policy.

Here is an example. When President Obama began campaigning for office in 2007, he pledged to close the military detainee camp at Guantanamo Bay, Cuba. He again declared his intention to do so during his first days as president in 2009. As of the writing of this text, "Gitmo" remains open and houses over 160 detainees. Why? There are a variety of reasons, but the largest is this: We don't know what to do with the prisoners incarcerated there. Title V, Section 530 of H.R. 933 Consolidated and Further Continuing Appropriations Act of 2013 prohibits the use of federal funds to transfer to the United States any prisoner currently at Guantanamo Bay. While there is no federal law preventing these transfers to U.S. prisons, without funding the detainees must remain where they are. This is policymaking via appropriations.

Public Law 107-40: Authorization for Use of Military Force

On September 18, 2001, the U.S. Congress passed a joint resolution authorizing the use of military force against those "nations, organizations, and persons" determined to have "planned, authorized, committed, or aided" the terrorist attacks of September 11th. Almost 13 years later, this **Authorization for the Use of Military Force** (AUMF) is still in effect and the scope has been expanded considerably. Initially intended as an authorization for the United States to strike at al-Qaeda and its supporters, the resolution was used as the basis for the invasion of Afghanistan, the war in Iraq, and ongoing drone strikes in many parts of the world.

The terms "nations, organizations, and persons" has, over the years, been interpreted to included anyone with terrorist intent against the United States, and targets of military force have included men who were only 7 or 8 years old at the time of the 9/11 attacks. It is difficult to extend the concept of assisting or carrying out the 9/11 attacks to persons who were in grade school at the time.

The AUMF has become a political issue for the United States, both domestically and internationally. In September 2010, Representative Barbara Lee, a

Democrat from California, introduced H.R. 6282, a bill to repeal the AUMF. Her bill was never brought before the full House for a vote; it died in committee. Rep. Lee reintroduced her bill as H.R. 2859 in September of 2011, where it also died without action, and again as H.R. 198 in January 2013. Again, the bill was not passed into law. These bills indicate some desire, politically, in the United States to eliminate the AUMF, but the simple reality is this: Without the authorization, most military counterterrorism activity overseas would become unauthorized and illegal and have to stop, including ongoing operations in Afghanistan. Despite the opposition to involvement in Afghanistan and ongoing drone strikes in foreign countries, these programs have been defined through 12 years of perception as our first line of defense against terrorism. In short, the AUMF provides the United States with a way to fight terrorist organizations overseas before they can reach American soil. So while the United States may want and need a more finely tuned method for authorizing direct counterterrorism operations, it cannot scrap the existing authorization until a replacement is passed into law.

USA PATRIOT Act

Within weeks of the 9/11 attacks, the U.S. Congress had drafted and passed the **USA PATRIOT ACT** to strengthen U.S. counterterrorism capabilities. Of course, the name of the act is an acronym; the full name is the Uniting and Strengthening America by Providing Appropriate Tools Required to Intercept and Obstruct Terrorism. Despite the long name, the acronym is typically ignored and the legislation is referred to as simply the PATRIOT ACT.

The bill was created in direct response to perceived shortcomings in the U.S. law enforcement and intelligence communities that failed to prevent 9/11. The PATRIOT ACT had bipartisan support and passed the U.S. Senate with a 98–1 vote and the House of Representatives with a 357–66 margin. President George W. Bush signed the bill into law, and civil rights groups immediately began talking about how the Act infringed upon the privacy and civil liberties of American citizens. In fact, this was the loudest conversation; the government was going to use the PATRIOT ACT to spy on citizens, outside of terrorism investigation. Where did these allegations come from?

The biggest complaints revolved around the PATRIOT ACT's provisions that gave new access to private business records, including sales receipts, bank records, and library information. In fact, the idea that the government could now track what citizens were checking out of libraries became the centerpiece of the civil liberty vs. security battle. The truth, however, is much less threatening. The core of the PATRIOT ACT is designed to allow investigators the ability to identify terrorists before they know they are being investigated. This secrecy prevents the would-be terrorist from destroying evidence or otherwise impeding the investigation and leads to a more complete picture of the threat the terrorist and/or organization poses.

If a person is suspected of committing fraud, or laundering money, federal law enforcement will want to look at business records and bank account information. To accomplish this in a simple criminal investigation, the prosecutor convenes a grand jury, a group of citizens that decides whether there is enough evidence to prosecute the accused for the crime. The grand jury may hear dozens of different cases during its session, and they have the power to issue subpoenas—documents that compel an individual to appear before the grand jury to give testimony. These subpoenas can also require specific documents or records be brought with the individual or produced separately. Simply put, if a prosecutor is assembling a criminal case against someone on fraud charges, they can already force individuals or organizations to surrender business records, bank statements, and library transactions. However, it is important to remember that the prosecutor cannot issue subpoenas; he or she must convince a jury of citizens that the information is pertinent and necessary. Only the grand jury has the power to compel testimony and evidence to appear.

In a national security case, the grand jury is not an appropriate tool for investigation and indictment. While grand jury proceedings are secret, it is made up of ordinary citizens, called to serve. They have no security clearance and cannot be fully briefed on government investigations and operations. Therefore, prior to the PATRIOT ACT, there was no secure mechanism for investigators and prosecutors to obtain business records from individuals suspected of being terrorists. The PATRIOT ACT changed that.

In national security cases, investigators can bypass the grand jury and petition the **Foreign Intelligence Surveillance Court** (FISC) for a subpoena to access business records. The FISC is a panel of federal judges that have been cleared to hear classified information, and was created in 1978 as part of the **Foreign Intelligence Surveillance Act**. FISA was designed to give federal investigators the power to conduct physical and electronic surveillance on persons and/or facilities of a **foreign power** for the purpose of collecting **foreign intelligence information**. It was part of the Cold War espionage and counterespionage "game" and was used extensively until the effective end of that conflict 20 years later. Many FISA searches and electronic surveillance could be carried out without a warrant, as long as the targets were foreign agents working inside the United States; it did not allow warrantless surveillance of American citizens. Surveillance operations against a foreign agent inside the United States could go on for up to one year without judicial review or a warrant. If the surveillance was to include a U.S. citizen inside the United States, a warrant must be obtained from a FISC judge within 72 hours after the surveillance begins.

So . . . what constitutes a foreign power under FISA? What about foreign intelligence information? A foreign power was defined (in 1978) as a foreign government, any faction of a foreign government or governments, any organization or entity directly acknowledged and controlled by a foreign government, or international terrorist organizations. Factions or entities of the foreign government could not be comprised of a majority of U.S. citizens, and international terrorist organizations were defined as operating outside of the United States. Foreign intelligence information is defined as information needed by the United States to protect against an actual or potential attack, sabotage, or acts of international terrorism. In 1978, these definitions were established without thought to the possibility of major terrorist attacks, without direct state support or control, inside the United States. As we entered the new era of terrorism, facing capable and determined enemies that operate across a spectrum of countries and regions, independent of the control or support of a foreign power, our legal framework for defense was outdated.

The PATRIOT ACT effectively amended FISA, and added terrorists and suspected terrorists inside the United States to the list of approved surveillance targets; it acknowledged that these actors may not have direct state sponsorship and were not controlled by a foreign power. The FISC could now issue orders to obtain the same types of records that a grand jury could subpoena, but without having to reveal classified or sensitive information to a civilian grand jury. Further, by expanding the list of approved surveillance targets initially defined in FISA, the PATRIOT ACT gave investigators the ability to conduct warrantless surveillance on persons suspected of terrorism as long as they were inside the United States and not a U.S. citizen.

So the PATRIOT ACT gave law enforcement and other investigators the ability to acquire surveillance information and records on suspected terrorists, but in reality this was not a great expansion of power, it simply streamlined the process and allowed the government to remain secretive about some activities. The secrecy alone is enough to worry some Americans, and perhaps rightfully so. However, the counterpoint is simple: The more we know about government activities, the more our opponents will know and that is not a good thing. One thing is certain, the debate on this point will continue for years to come.

What else did the PATRIOT ACT do? Outside of the expansion and modification of surveillance activity, it allowed for better information sharing between investigators and agencies. Prior to the PATRIOT ACT, information gathered during the course of an FBI criminal investigation could not be shared with FBI investigators working a national security or terrorism case. This "wall" between the two types of cases in the FBI (criminal and national security) was created through administrative interpretations of statute and policy; there was no explicit prohibition on information sharing. The practice stemmed from the fact that during a criminal investigation, all evidence collected must be ready to present in court, while the same was not true for evidence and information collected in a national security case. These differing standards led to a fear that mixing the information could lead to failed prosecutions. This wall had a direct impact on 9/11, as investigators working criminal fraud and money laundering investigations had information that pertained to the 19 hijackers in the United States. The wall prevented them from sharing this information with investigators and analysts working counter-terrorism. To be clear, there was no "smoking gun" evidence in the possession of the criminal case investigators that if shared would have prevented the 9/11 attacks, but the art of intelligence analysis requires as much information and data as possible to build a picture of what is happening now, so that future activity can be extrapolated. If you think that last phrase sounds complicated, that is nothing compared to actually trying to accomplish the task.

While civil liberty activists and the media talked about the expanded surveillance powers granted by the PATRIOT ACT, very few discussed the information sharing mandates in the law . . . and that is the most important part! The surveillance provisions are important and effective (and not a true erosion of privacy) but useless without the ability to build a complete picture of terrorist operations in and pertaining to the United States. The national discussion was controlled by fear, not by what was truly important.

Sanctions

In 2002, President Bush defined the "Axis of Evil" as the nations of Iraq, Iran, and North Korea. He accused these nations of supporting and encouraging international terrorism as well as attempting to acquire the capability to build and deploy weapons of mass destruction. The next year, the Bush Administration would invade Iraq to eliminate the threat of Saddam Hussein's regime toward the United States (only after the fact would the Iraqi threat be exposed as false).

Sanctions against Iran

The United States has supported economic sanctions against Iran since 1987. At that time, citing support of terrorism and belligerent actions against neutral shipping in the Persian Gulf, U.S. President Ronald Reagan prohibited the import to the United States of all Iranian goods and services, including petroleum. In 1995, President Clinton strengthened the sanctions by prohibiting U.S. firms and companies from participating in oil exploration or development in Iran.

However, the sanctions have had little impact on the foreign policy of Iran, or how it behaves toward the United States. Like all economic sanctions, impacts are felt by the middle class and the poor, not the ruling elite. This fosters grassroots level animosity toward the sanctioning country, and this is true in Iran. Public support for softening of relations toward the United States has eroded as economic impacts are felt across the country. Without domestic pressure to change policy (not that it would be all that effective anyway), there is reduced incentive for the targeted country to change.

While the United States outlawed the import of Iranian oil, other countries did not follow suit. With ready buyers in Europe and Asia, the Iranian oil industry was far from crippled by the U.S. actions.

(Continued)

In 2008, Iran restarted its nuclear development program. While they publicly declared the research was aimed at creating nuclear reactors for generating electricity, much of the world did not approve of this nuclear proliferation. In 2008 and 2009 revised U.S. sanctions were put into place that prohibited U.S. banks from transferring money to any bank that had any tie to Iran—even if the source and destination banks were not Iranian institutions. All exceptions to import sanctions, mainly regarding food and rugs, were cancelled, all in an effort to convince Iran to abandon its nuclear program.

Despite the U.S. sanctions, Iran continued to sponsor (and still sponsors) international terrorism in Lebanon and Palestine through donations of money, material, and training to Hezbollah and Hamas. Again, U.S. sanctions were not effective in controlling unwanted and hostile foreign actions.

In 2012, the European Union (finally) joined the embargo on Iranian oil, again to pressure the Iranian government to suspend nuclear research and cease supporting Hezbollah and Hamas. As of this writing, this has reduced annual Iranian oil revenue by over 40%, as their remaining markets (primarily China, Russia, and other Asian destinations) do not have the demand to receive the excess oil normally sold to Europe. For once, Western sanctions are truly hurting Iran. However, the Iranian government and people view their nuclear program as a point of national defense and national pride and there are no signs they are close to abandoning nuclear development in light of international economic pressure.

Prior to military action such as the 2003 invasion of Iraq, what recourse do nations have to prevent a "rogue" nation from acting in an inappropriate way? In other words, how do you keep the Irans and Iraqs of the world from sponsoring terrorism? Aside from stern language or military action, the only real option is **economic sanctions**. Sanctions are internationally recognized penalties applied to a country by another country or group of countries. Sanctions usually economically harmful to the targeted country, and are designed to either punish or force policy agreement and/or cooperation. To be effective, the sanction should create a significant impact on the target country's economy and should not be something that can be easily bypassed. For example, if Country Able is supporting terrorism and Country Baker disapproves, Baker may put a trade embargo in effect that prohibits the purchase of goods from Able. Of course, this is only effective if Baker is a significant trading partner with Able, and there are no other un-embargoed markets for Country Able's goods. If Countries Charlie and David wish to trade with Able and continue to do so after Baker puts the sanctions into place, the embargo will not have as severe an impact and may not drive the cooperation intended. Even if an embargo is effective economically, that does not mean it will accomplish what was intended.

Palestinian Sanctions

The Palestinian Territories are divided across two separate geographic areas, the West Bank, situated east of Jerusalem between Israel and Jordan, and the Gaza Strip, located in the extreme south west of Israel, along the coast of the Mediterranean and adjacent to Egypt. In 2006, the terrorist group turned political party Hamas won a majority of the seats in the Palestinian parliamentary elections and moved to form a government. Clearly, Israel and the United States were less then thrilled with a terrorist organization (it's slightly more complicated than that, but stick with me here . . .) creating a government in any part of Palestine, so both countries (as well as the EU and most Arab nations) put economic sanctions into place and suspended all foreign aid into the Gaza strip. This type of sanction was harsher than simply preventing trade with a target nation. The Palestinian National Authority depended on foreign aid as the primary revenue of the government, and basic government services were funded through these mechanisms; without a flow of foreign cash, the new government would be unable to function. The Hamas led government did not last long. In late 2006 and throughout 2007, Fatah, the political wing of the Palestinian Liberation Organization (PLO) that had controlled parliament before the election, escalated their war of words with Hamas into a shooting conflict. The Gaza War in the summer of 2007 saw Hamas eject Fatah representatives and supporters from Gaza and Fatah established control in the West Bank.

In 2012, talks began again between the two parties, and they have announced their intention to form a coalition government. Since the Gaza War, the Fatah controlled West Bank has seen some relaxations on sanctions, while the Hamas controlled Gaza strip remains cut off from the outside world. If these two parties form a new coalition Palestinian government, it will have to tread carefully on how it acts toward Israel. A hardline approach, such as what Hamas has advertised for the last six years, will see a new round of international condemnation and sanctions.

How can the United States and other nations target one part of Palestine (Gaza) more than another (the West Bank)? Unlike Iran or other targeted nations, there are not blanket U.S. sanctions against the Palestinian National Authority or Palestinian Territories. Remember, foreign aid for sources such as the U.S. government, as well as private charities in the United States and elsewhere, are a huge part of Palestinian revenue. To control the flow of money and goods into Palestine, the United States has invoked the U.S. Terrorism Sanction Regulations, first established in September 2001. Under that regulation, U.S. entities are forbidden to trade with or financially support dozens of specific organizations and charities in the Palestinian Territories. The U.S. State Department and the Department of the Treasury can modify this list of forbidden entities nearly at will, providing granular control over where money can and cannot flow.

The issue of the Palestinian territories will not be solved overnight, and we are headed into a new era as Gaza and the West Bank move toward a unified government and resume diplomatic relations with Israel.

The most famous U.S. sanction is the Cuba trade embargo that has been in place since July 1963. Officially known as the Cuban Assets Control Regulations, these federal laws prohibit travel to and from Cuba by U.S. citizens as well as the import or export of goods or materials to and from Cuba or Cuban companies. While the Cuban trade embargo has been in effect for almost 60 years, no political or social changes have been brought on by the sanction.

While Americans are prohibited from travel to and from Cuba, and cannot buy Cuban cigars or other goods, those restrictions are not true for any other nation in the world. Canadians can travel to Cuba and purchase goods; Mexicans, Germans, and Chinese (as well as just about every other nation on Earth) can all do the same. While the United States represents a massive trading partner for any country, and is located in close proximity to Cuba, it is clear that the U.S. embargo did not have enough of an economic effect to change internal Cuban policy or government.

Domestic and Local Counterterrorism Efforts

Counterterrorism in our current era involves every level of government, the private sector, and the average citizen. The United States quickly realized that the public and local government were untapped resources in the effort to stop terrorism, and numerous efforts have been undertaken since 9/11 to involve those populations and organizations.

Public Engagement

In the current era of terrorism, citizens around the world have become involved in the efforts to fight terror and extremism. In the United States terrorism seems like a new phenomenon, but that isn't really the case—Americans are just relatively new to dealing with terrorist attacks on their soil.

Why do we need the public to be involved in counterterrorism? Two reasons. First, engaging the public in preparedness and prevention activities provides an outlet for anxiety and uncertainty; people feel better when they can exert some measure of control. As an example, the American Red Cross provides simple ways for people to prepare for a terrorist attack including family communications plans and lists of what to expect after an attack. This type of information allows citizens to better understand the reality of what could happen during an attack, and even if the preparedness steps are never used, they give a sense of security and reduce stress about uncertainty (American Red Cross, 2013). The American Psychological Association provides resources for citizens on dealing with the trauma of a terrorist attack. Again, this provides a level of understanding for citizens about what to except in the aftermath of an attack (Fields & Margolin, 2001).

Sami Osmakac

In January 2012, the FBI arrested 25-year-old Sami Osmakac in Tampa, Florida. He was planning attacks against nightclubs and law enforcement in Tampa and had been in contact with an undercover agent to purchase explosives and weapons. How did he get in touch with the undercover agent in the first place?

Osmakac is an American citizen who was born in the former Yugoslavia. He and his family were practicing Muslims, and he was vocal in his protests about the local government and Christians. Prior to these events, he posted several videos to You-Tube advocating his views, and had had several run-ins with local law enforcement and citizens. As he developed these plans to attack Tampa, he hinted at them to the other members of his mosque . . . and they called the FBI.

The FBI began an investigation and put an agent in touch with Osmakac. When the plans developed to the point that he attempted to purchase an AK-47, an Uzi submachine gun, and an explosive device from the agent, he was arrested. This event is not out of the ordinary. Local communities are the best defense we have against terrorism, particularly these single actor scenarios, and these communities have shown again and again their willingness to participate in counterterrorism efforts.

The second reason we need to engage the public in counterterrorism operations is simple: information. The public has it, and counterterrorism officials need it. This is the basis behind the "See Something, Say Something" campaign; encourage the public to come forward with information that may help us defend against attacks. The reality is that community information is effective in combatting all types of crime and threats, including terrorism. The number of ordinary citizens who are moving through communities every minute of every day dwarfs the relatively small number of law enforcement officers in the United States. Ordinary citizens will often encounter crucial pieces of information; when this information is provided to authorities they are then able to construct a more complete picture of potential terrorist activity.

Citizen engagement is two-way communication. The public needs preparedness information about terrorist threats, and government needs information about what is happening in the community. When both of these channels are working effectively, both the community and counterterrorism efforts are better prepared.

Crowdsourcing Counterterrorism

When two explosive devices exploded at the finish line of the 2013 Boston Marathon, the entire world was watching. Multiple television networks had cameras running, and the explosions were captured from several angles and vantage points. Bystanders and race fans used cell phones to take pictures and video, even some runners had strapped on video cameras for the race. Surveillance cameras, some belonging to retail and hospitality venues near the finish line, as well as some traffic monitoring cameras, dutifully recorded images from before, during, and after the detonations. In short, the event was extremely well-documented.

Boston Police and the FBI requested anyone with photos or videos of the area submit them to the authorities for analysis—even if the images came from hours before the attacks. Investigators wanted to piece together these thousands of sources into a timeline showing as many people as possible. Obviously, the bomber or bombers were present, and it was assumed that someone had captured a photo or video of the perpetrators. It was just a matter of teasing out the terrorists from the crowd.

As investigators began this process, the Internet joined the search. People from all over the world combed through the published photos of the event, looking for suspects. Crime scene photos released by the FBI showed the tattered remains of a black backpack—the container for one of the improvised weapons. Immediately, photos of men carrying black backpacks near the blast site flooded message boards and social media sites, and at least one print newspaper in New York published a photo on the front page asking "Have You Seen These Men?" All of this occurred a day before the FBI would finally release pictures of the two real suspects, the Tsarnaev brothers.

This is, in effect, crowdsourcing counterterrorism. By engaging the public and making specific requests for information (pictures and video), investigators were tapping a massive resource of information.

Three days after the attacks, law enforcement released photos of two suspects, taken from a combination of surveillance cameras and bystander snapshots. While they had photos, they did not have names. Identification did not take long as dozens of people called into report they knew the Tsarnaev brothers. Again, this call for assistance put the power to "do something" in the public's hands—and it was very effective. The brothers were identified and eventually killed (one) and captured (one) due to public participation in the counterterrorism effort.

Pseudo-Security

While terrorism remains a threat to modern society, how big of a threat is it? If you look at the amount of money spent, the political emphasis, and the scope of counterterrorism operations at all levels of government, you would expect that terrorism kills or maims hundreds or thousands of people per year. It doesn't. Between 2010 and 2011, approximately 25,000 people were killed worldwide in terrorist attacks. Of those, only 32 were Americans, and all of those were killed outside the United States. By comparison, in the same time period it is estimated that almost 300 Americans were killed by furniture or a television falling on them. Further, approximately 23,000 Americans a year die from alcohol related incidents, and 18,000 Americans are murdered each year. Clearly, the threat to human life is greater from whiskey distilleries than from terrorists, but we don't act that way. This irrational fear of terrorism comes from many places, most of which are better left to a psychology text. And don't read too much into our flimsy comparisons, they are illustrative, not political.

The new era of terrorism could also be called the era of **pseudo-security**: Actions we take and policies we write that make us "feel" safer, but don't actually increase our safety or security. It is false security, undertaken to make us as a population "feel better" —the government is "doing something" to make us more secure.

Examples of these abound. When you go into a local government office or building, you have to sign in and produce identification. This process is overseen by either a low-level administrative assistant or a private security guard. Showing identification and signing a sheet is not going to deter or prevent a terrorist attack on the building or its occupants. Parking or waiting in front of an airport terminal became a traffic violation in many jurisdictions after 9/11. The official explanation is that this is to deter terrorists with car bombs. Really? The threat of a $50 ticket is enough to deter or prevent a terrorist from detonating an explosive in front of the airport? Many of these types of policies are put in place in the name of the dangers of terrorism, yet assume that we are facing terrorists that aren't smart or who have a plan. Policymaking is often a hotbed of irony.

Society needs to shake the overwhelming fear of terrorism and realize that we are spending money on things (such as rental guards on front desks and "no parking" signs) that do not make us safer at all. In fact, by making us think that terrorism is such a constant threat that the local board of education needs a rent-a-cop inflates the capability and menace of our enemies.

Expanded Intelligence Gathering

If you want to know what is happening regarding drug trafficking, fencing of stolen goods, or car thefts in a mid-sized American town, whom do you contact? The FBI? No. You call the local police department. Local law enforcement has more information on patterns, trends, and crime in their jurisdiction than anyone else. In the past 10 years, local law enforcement data has begun to be included in the overall national counterterrorism and intelligence gathering operations. If a terrorist or terrorist organization is using local crime to finance operations, the best way to gather that information is through the local law enforcement agencies. If local drug traffic is happening in conjunction with or in support of a terrorist organization, local law enforcement information and data is the best way to understand this.

Local law enforcement intelligence is fed up from the local level to state-wide or regional **fusion centers**. In these fusion centers, analysts look at reports and patterns of criminal behavior or activity and link it to potential terrorism or national security concerns. Analyzed information (intelligence) is passed from the state fusion center upward to the national- or federal-level agencies or federal fusion centers. Further, information of importance to the local authorities is passed from the national level down to the local level through the fusion center.

Anti-Terrorism and Countering Violent Extremism (CVE)

We have talked quite a bit throughout this book about counterterrorism—fighting terrorists directly and making it more difficult from them to attack us. The majority of our policy and direct efforts fall into this category. What about efforts to prevent terrorists from radicalizing in the first place? Can we prevent extremists from wanting to attack us? Those efforts are bundled under the auspices of **anti-terrorism**.

The 2011 National Strategy for Counter-Terrorism defined eight goals in combatting terrorism domestically and abroad. Number seven in the list is titled, *Counter al-Qa'ida Ideology and Its Resonance and Diminish the Specific Drivers of Violence that al-Qa'ida Exploits*. This goal recognizes the need to prevent terrorists from radicalizing in the first place. As we discussed in Chapter 2, terrorists radicalize and choose a path of violence for several reasons, among them is the view that violence and their cause is legitimate. They create that view of legitimacy through a variety of means, and we must counter this view with long-term polices and programs that build resilience to violent messages. The strategy document states:

> " *Along with the majority of people across all religious and cultural traditions, we aim for a world in which al-Qa'ida is openly and widely rejected by all audiences as irrelevant to their aspirations and concerns, a world where al-Qa'ida's ideology does not shape perceptions of world and local events, inspire violence, or serve as a recruiting tool for the group or its adherents. Although achieving this objective is likely to require a concerted long-term effort, we must retain a focus on addressing the near-term challenge of preventing those individuals already on the brink from embracing al-Qa'ida ideology and resorting to violence. We will work closely with local and global partners, inside and outside governments, to discredit al-Qa'ida ideology and reduce its resonance. We will put forward a positive vision of engagement with foreign publics and support for universal rights that demonstrates that the United States aims to build while al-Qa'ida would only destroy. We will apply focused foreign and development assistance abroad. At the same time, we will continue to assist, engage, and connect communities to increase their collective resilience abroad and at home. These efforts strengthen bulwarks against radicalization, recruitment, and mobilization to violence in the name of al-Qa'ida and will focus in particular on those drivers that we know al-Qa'ida exploits. (The White House, 2011)* " "

Terrorists in the modern era are using the Internet to spread messages of violence and hate; the Web has become a breeding ground and recruitment tool for violent extremism. At a security conference in 2012, it was discussed that there were over 17,000 websites that promote jihad, terrorism, or violence. The United States actively managed fewer than 20 to counter this prolific message. That ratio is terrible and needs to be addressed.

However, countering violent extremism (CVE) efforts cannot come from government sources. I'm sure you have all heard the tongue-in-cheek phrase: "I'm from the government and I'm here to help you." The sarcasm in that snippet stems from the fact that very rarely is that 100% true—and when it is, government efforts often do not meet the needs of the people being assisted.

Take that attitude into Pakistan, into Afghanistan, into Saudi Arabia, into Iraq . . . As a representative of a Western government, how much credibility to you have trying to convince a 21-year-old native of those regions that everything he has been told about America, about the West, how we are trying to destroy his culture and his religion, how the only way to fight us is with terrorism, is *wrong*? Will that potential terrorist trust your message? Will he believe that the West doesn't want any of those things? Or will he believe that your efforts are more lies and deceit, and turn his back on you?

The only effective CVE must come from within the community itself, not from the government. This is true even here in the United States. Our largest threat from terrorism lies in the "homegrown" extremist, and our communities are our best defense against these threats. Youth groups, community organizations, and religious institutions are forming the front line against radicalization. In many ways, CVE is easier here at home than it is abroad. In the United States, citizens have outlets for frustrations and anger toward the government. Elections are free, and speech is protected. These factors reduce the allure of radicalization and violence—for most. In other societies, where the freedoms that American's take for granted are not present, where poverty is rampant and oppressive, and where governments are corrupt and unconcerned—these are the areas where radicalization blooms and terrorism takes root. Unfortunately, Western values and culture are often blamed for conditions in poor parts of the world, and some of that may be true. The West exports food, culture, movies, music, fashion, cars, and innumerable other material and social goods, but these luxuries are forever out of reach to all but a very few wealthy people. This inability to define a path to achieve these Western goods and values creates resentment, which in turn drives people toward other paths to—they turn to extremism and terrorism.

Countering this radicalization ultimately requires education and outreach—much like community based counterterrorism. Radicalization can be slowed or halted by members of the would-be terrorists' community, not by foreign government. Embracing and encouraging that is something governments around the world need to foster.

Key Terms

Anti-terrorism

Appropriations bill

Authorization for the Use of Military Force

Continuing resolution

Economic sanctions

Foreign intelligence information

Foreign Intelligence Surveillance Act

Foreign Intelligence Surveillance Court

Foreign power

Fusion center

Pseudo-security

USA PATRIOT ACT

Discussion Questions

1. Should sanctions be applied to terrorism supporting countries in cases where the government is not elected by or persuaded by the people?

2. Is FISA the appropriate legal mechanism for fighting terrorism at home, or should investigators use more traditional techniques?

References

107th Congress. (2001). *Public Law 107-40.* United States Congress. Washington, D.C.: Congressional Record.

American Red Cross. (2013, January 1). *Terrorism preparedness*. Retrieved March 14, 2013, from American Red Cross: www.redcross.org/prepare/disaster/terrorism

Coburn, Tom. Safety at any price: Assessing the impact of Homeland Security spending in U.S. cities. December 2012, Office of Senator Tom Coburn. Homeland Security and Governmental Affairs Committee.

Federal Emergency Management Agency. (2013, May 20). *FY 2013 Homeland Security Grant Program (HSGP)*. Retrieved May 25, 2013, from Federal Emergency Management Agency: www.fema.gov/fy-2013-homeland-security-grant-program-hsgp-0

Fields, R. M., & Margolin, J. (2001, September 30). *Managing traumatic stress: Coping with terrorism*. Retrieved May 12, 2013, from American Psychological Association: www.apa.org/helpcenter/terrorism.aspx

Office of Foreign Assets Control. (2001). *Terrorism sanctions regulations, Title 31 Part 595 of the U.S. Code of Federal Regulations.* Washington, DC: U.S. Department of the Treasury.

Office of Foreign Assets Control. (2013, May 23). *Sanctions programs and country information*. Retrieved May 25, 2013, from U.S. Department of the Treasury: www.treasury.gov/resource-center/sanctions/Programs/Pages/Programs.aspx

S. 645—113th Congress: Refugee Protection Act of 2013. (2013). In www.GovTrack.us. Retrieved May 24, 2013, from www.govtrack.us/congress/bills/113/s645

The White House. (2011). *National strategy for counterterrorism, June 2011*. Washington, DC: The White House.

U.S. Census Bureau. (2007). *Death and death rates by selected causes.* Washington, DC: U.S. Census Bureau.

U.S. Department of Justice. (2001). *The USA PATRIOT ACT: Preserving life and liberty*. Washington, DC: U.S. Department of Justice.

CPSIA information can be obtained
at www.ICGtesting.com
Printed in the USA
LVHW101606010819
626173LV00001B/1/P

9 781465 234902